Let's Pretend

50 Start-to-Finish Preschooler Programs for the Busy Librarian That Foster Imagination

R E B E C C A   C .   B A N E

Neal-Schuman Publishers, Inc.

New York   London

Published by Neal-Schuman Publishers, Inc.
100 William St., Suite 2004
New York, NY 10038

Printed and bound in the United States of America.

The paper used in this publication meets the minimum requirements of American National Standard for Information Sciences—Permanence of Paper for Printed Library Materials, ANSI Z39.48-1992.

Library of Congress Cataloging-in-Publication Data

Bane, Rebecca C., 1978-
    Let's pretend : 50 start-to-finish preschooler programs for the busy librarian that foster imagination / Rebecca C. Bane.
        p. cm.
    Includes bibliographical references and index.
    ISBN 978-1-55570-728-6 (alk. paper)
    1. Children's libraries—Activity programs—United States. 2. Libraries and preschool children—United States. 3. Storytelling—United States. 4. Imagination in children. I. Title.

Z718.3.B36 2010
027.62'51—dc22
                                                                2010029956

This book is dedicated to:

Ean and Ivy, my children;
may you always look
to your imagination for inspiration.

Karen Allen, who has been an inspiration to me,
gave me the opportunity to start the "Let's Pretend" program,
and encouraged me to write about it.

Sandra, my imaginary childhood friend,
who helped me to discover
the world of imagination.

Table of Contents

Preface

I cannot tell you what my favorite toy was as a child, but I can tell you what my favorite pastime was: I loved to pretend. My world revolved around make-believe play. For as long as I can remember, I would invite anyone around me, including Sandra, my imaginary friend, to "Let's pretend that...," and there I would open the door to the world of imagination. One day my aunt asked me, "Pretend? How do you know what that word means?" Even at a very young age, when my vocabulary probably wasn't that well developed, I knew what the word "pretend" meant, and I knew how to do it.

Unfortunately, the door to the world of imagination for today's children, while not completely shut, seems to be only slightly ajar. Their lives are structured around schedules, with little room for open-ended play. Their toys are battery-operated mechanisms. As I look in my own one-year-old's toy box, I see more toys with batteries than not. Yes, these toys have fancy lights and sounds that offer instant gratification and capture his attention immediately, but that's about where the "play" ends. Soon enough, he loses interest, especially when the batteries die and the toy doesn't have much left to offer. However, give him a book with a variety of pictures and textures, a ball to throw or put in and out of containers, or even a paper towel roll or box, and he is entertained for much longer. Honestly, he would rather play with the boxes his toys came in than with the toys themselves. He can push the box around, fill it up with various items he collects as he makes his way around the room, and sit inside it with an expression of pure bliss while Mommy drags him around in this new "vehicle." The ways to play with items such as boxes are endless. Children thrive on this type of open-ended play, even at very young ages.

Why This Book and What's in the Book?

Working with children on a daily basis in the Youth Services Department of the Greenville County (SC) Library System put me back in touch with my inner child and placed me at the forefront of thinking creatively for children's sake in developing library programs. Thus, I developed "Let's Pretend" programs that use books, songs, fingerplays, flannel board stories, and props to guide children through play that focuses on the imagination and fosters the development of thinking, language, social, and physical skills. The programs consist of a modified storytime that introduces children to the pretend play that follows the story. *Let's Pretend: 50 Start-to-Finish Preschooler Programs for the Busy Librarian That Foster Imagination* brings together 50 fun and exciting "Let's Pretend" programs for readers to use and adapt to their own storytime program.

Storytime programs consist of books, songs, fingerplays, flannel board presentations, and puppets. In a traditional storytime program setting, the children are usually seated in front of the presenter as they listen to stories and then participate in action rhymes and songs between stories. A dramatic play program expands on this standard to introduce new concepts which children are encouraged to embrace with their imaginations. Each program of *Let's Pretend* outlines a way to present a particular theme, including possible book titles, music, songs, fingerplays, flannel board stories, props to make, and how to guide the children through play.

Each program is structured to include all of the information that you will need to present a "Let's Pretend" program:

- **Introduction**—sets the stage for the program, giving the setting for each of the "Let's Pretend" activities.
- **Materials Needed**—consists of three parts:
  - ◦ **Props**—lists all of the props that will be used along with instructions of how to create them using inexpensive, everyday materials.
  - ◦ **Books**—lists suggested books to be read during the program.
  - ◦ **Music**—lists songs/music to be played during the program.
- **A Step-by-Step Program Example**—guides the reader through each step of a possible "Let's Pretend" program, from start to finish.
- **Additional Props**—lists some additional props to consider, including instructions for making them.
- **Final Thoughts**—each "Let's Pretend" program ends with this list of developmental skills that children will learn through the program.
- **Photographs**—so that you'll be able to see what I'm describing, all programs are illustrated with color photographs showing props and program setup or children playing "Let's Pretend."

Let's Pretend contains 50 programs for preschoolers, for use by busy librarians, teachers, caregivers, or daycare personnel, which give complete, start-to-finish instructions for presenting imaginative storytime experiences. Through the use of inexpensive, everyday materials for props and the use of imaginative play, this book will introduce preschoolers to everything from day-to-day chores and activities (e.g., in the kitchen, house, around town, pizza parlor) to people (e.g., firefighters, pirates, doctors, construction workers), to special events (e.g., a parade, birthday party, dog show, spring picnic), to adventures (e.g., under the sea, outer space, boat trip, dinosaur dig, jungle safari), to nature (e.g., rainy day, apple farm, beach, garden, mountains, pond), to just plain imagination (e.g., haunted house, Land of Mother Goose, World of Pure Imagination).

The Literacy Connection

Children work really hard at playing. That's their job. It is a challenging experience because they are learning to think creatively, solve problems, communicate, develop physical skills, and learn about the world around them. During dramatic play, a child has the ability to shape his or her own world. Educators and psychologists have conducted numerous studies and research on the importance of imaginative play and its effects on a child's development. According to Doris Bergen (2002), a professor of educational psychology at Miami University in Oxford, Ohio, "There is a growing body of evidence to suggest that high-quality pretend play is an important facilitator of perspective taking and later abstract thought, that it may facilitate higher-level cognition and linguistic competence." Albert Einstein was aware of this during his lifetime, as he stated that "imagination is more important than knowledge" (BrainyQuote.com). Children do need education, but this can begin with the imagination, as L. Frank Baum (1998) states in the introduction to *The Lost Princess of Oz*:

> Imagination has given us the steam engine, the telephone, the talking-machine and the automobile, for these things had to be dreamed of before they became realities. So I believe that dreams—day dreams, you know, with your eyes wide open and your brain-machinery whizzing—are likely to lead to the betterment of the world. The imaginative child will become the imaginative man or woman most apt to create, to invent, and therefore to foster civilization. (p. 13)

Using books with imaginative play is a great way to foster literacy development and a love for reading. A child with a rich imagination develops an ongoing curiosity, which creates a desire to gain knowledge. One of the best ways to gain knowledge is through reading. In turn, reading books opens up many avenues to explore the world through pretend play. In his article, "The Magic of Make-Believe," David McKay Wilson (2005) states that books give a base knowledge about the world and provide inspiration a child needs to make up his or her own thoughts "(she can't pretend she's a space traveler or a ballerina unless she knows what an astronaut or a dancer does)." Thus, books and the imagination, developed through pretend play, foster literacy development. That's what makes a dramatic play storytime program ideal for libraries, day care facilities, preschools, and anyone caring for children. Parents and caregivers can also benefit from the themes presented in the following programs because the ideas offer ways to use common household items as playthings, creating a bonding experience as the child and adult use their imaginations to make things together.

Budget- and Environmentally-Friendly Programming

Not only is imaginative play great for fostering child development and literacy, it is also economical and environmentally friendly. Rather than buying a plastic fire truck that will eventually end up in a landfill, why not save that large box waiting to be discarded? With that box, you not only have a fire truck, but also a bus, train, or any other vehicle. Need binoculars for a "nature walk"? Save up toilet paper rolls and attach a piece of yarn. Voila! You can spend a little extra money to dress up these props, but it is not necessary. A child can look at a box and see a fire truck, if that's what he or she desires it to be. However, it is fun to get creative with arts and crafts, especially when children are helping. Even if you do decide to get crafty, a few craft supplies are much cheaper than buying a new toy for every type of playtime. By reusing what you have at home or work, you are also reducing waste.

Conclusion

A dramatic play storytime may appear to be much more work than a traditional storytime but, really, it's only a storytime with dramatic playtime added. Depending on the number of children who will be participating, you will need time to collect enough prop-making supplies. You also have to determine how fancy you want to make the props and allow time to make them. However, the actual storytime requires less preparation and planning, as it will be shorter than most storytimes. I have included 50 different themes, but you will soon realize that any storytime theme can be turned into dramatic play. All that is required is a little creative thinking and lots of fun.

I hope that you will enjoy these dramatic play programs as much as I have. It is fun to plan and prepare each theme, but the most fun is in the presentation, when the program comes alive. The joy that each child brings into each program is the greatest delight of all.

References

Baum, L. Frank. 1998. "To My Readers." *The Lost Princess of Oz*. New York: Harper-Collins.

Bergen, Doris. 2002. "The Role of Pretend Play in Children's Cognitive Development," *Early Childhood Research & Practice* 4, no. 1 (Spring). Available: ecrp.uiuc.edu/v4n1/bergen.html (accessed June 1, 2010).

BrainyQuote.com. "Albert Einstein Quotes." Available: www.brainyquote.com/quotes/authors/a/albert_ einstein_4.html (accessed June 1, 2010).

Wilson, David McKay. 2005. "The Magic of Make-Believe." *Parents* 80, no. 4 (April). Available: www.parents.com/parents/story.jsp?storyid+/templatedata/parents/story/data/6008.xml (accessed June 1, 2010).

Acknowledgments

I owe many thanks to the following people:

Gail Moore for contributing to an article that opened the door for a book about "Let's Pretend."

Jennifer Pinkerman and Vanessa Ayers for helping me during "Let's Pretend" programs and contributing to its success.

Leigh Ramey for continuing the "Let's Pretend" program and providing support for this book.

The Greenville County Library's Youth Services department for contributing their "trash" for "Let's Pretend" props.

Tab Wilson, a dear friend who helped me find time to finish this book.

Angie Collins for being a wonderful mother who has always fed my creativity.

Jason Bane, my wonderful husband and father to my children, who I cannot thank enough for his time and patience with me and our children during the writing process. I am blessed because he is the best.

Let's Pretend: Going Camping

Overview

Camping is an activity that engages the essence of nature. What better way to take a step back and enjoy the outdoors than by breathing in the fresh air of the woods and sleeping under the stars? Even if you cannot get away to the real outdoors, you can go there using your imagination. "Let's Pretend: Going Camping" offers ideas on how to take children on a camping trip without setting foot outside by using books, songs/music and other activities about camping, outdoor activities, forest animals, and the night sky.

Materials Needed

Props

Campfire: real firewood or paper towel rolls; red, yellow, and orange tissue paper

> Arrange firewood or paper towel rolls as you would when building a real fire. Stuff red, yellow, and orange tissue paper in the "wood" for "flames." Build the campfire near the tent area (see Figure 1.1).

Fish Pond: blue poster board or butcher paper, construction paper, magnets

> Cut a large piece of poster board or butcher paper to look like the shape of a pond. Cut the construction paper into fish shapes. Glue a magnet on the back of each fish. Place them in the "pond" (see Figure 1.2).

Fishing Poles: dowels, string, paper clip

> Tie a string around the end of the dowel. Tie a paper clip to the end of the string.

Trees: brown and green butcher paper or poster board

> Cut the brown paper into tree trunk shapes and the green paper into bushy tree top shapes. Place the green "foliage" at the top of the trunk. Make various sizes and tape them to the wall.

Figure 1.1. A campfire perfect for stories and a sing-a-long

Figure 1.2. Let's fish!

Pictures of Forest Animals

Binoculars: toilet paper rolls, yarn

> Attach yarn to two toilet paper rolls by punching a hole in each roll and making a knot in the yarn to keep it from sliding through the hole (see Figure 16.3, p. 46).

Figure 1.3. Looking for animals

Nature Trail: trees (see above) and forest animal pictures (see above)

Arrange trees along a wall and place the forest animal pictures in various locations. Use the binoculars (see above) to "search" for the animals (see Figure 1.3).

Starmaker: flashlight, black construction paper

Poke small holes into a piece of black construction paper and fit it over a flashlight. The holes can be punched out into a design (such as a constellation) or randomly placed.

Tent: blankets/sheets and chairs

Drape blankets and sheets over chairs to make a tent.

Miscellaneous: tent, stuffed animals, backpack, and anything else on hand that is camping and/or outdoor related

Books

Brillhart, Julie. *When Daddy Took Us Camping.* Morton Grove, IL: Albert Whitman & Company, 1997.

Ward, Jennifer. *Forest Bright/Forest Night.* Nevada City, NV: Dawn Publications, 2005.

Music

"A Camping We Will Go." *Barney's Favorites, Volume 1* [CD]. New York: SBK Records, 1993.

Allard, Peter T., and Ellen Allard. "Hello Everybody." *Sing It! Say It! Stamp It! Sway It! Volume 1* [CD]. Worcester, MA: 80-Z Music, 1999.

Moo, Anna. "Fireflies." *Anna Moo Crackers* [CD]. Newberry, FL: A. Music Productions, 1994.

Other

"Campfire Pokey"

You put your marshmallow in. / You take your marshmallow out.

You put your marshmallow in and you shake it all about.

You do the campfire pokey and you turn yourself about.

That's what it's all about!

For the remaining verses, substitute marshmallow with hot dog, potato, popcorn, and anything else that you can roast over the fire.

"Twinkle, Twinkle, Little Star"

Going Camping: A Step-by-Step Program Example

1. Opening song: "Hello Everybody."
2. Camping talk: Talk about camping with the children. Ask them questions such as:
   • How do you camp? (sleep out under the stars or in a tent)
   • What do you do when you camp? (pitch a tent, walk nature trails, fish, cook over a fire, etc.)

- What do you bring when you camp? (tent, sleeping bag, backpack, binoculars, first aid kit, etc.) or you could have a backpack filled with various items (camping and noncamping) and ask which ones you would bring on a camping trip).
3. Read *When Daddy Took Us Camping*.
4. Sing "A-Camping We Will Go."
5. Pitch a tent. Let the children make a tent with sheets/blankets and chairs.
6. Campfire time! Bring everyone back to the campfire and do the "Campfire Pokey."
7. Now it's time to eat! Take the children "fishing" at the "pond." As each child catches fish, let the child "cook" it over the "fire."
8. Read *Forest Bright/Forest Night*.
9. Let's take a nature walk! Now that the children are familiar with forest animals, give them "binoculars" and let them go on the "nature trail."
10. It's nighttime! Dim the lights and bring everyone back to the camping area. Ask them "What comes out at night, glows, and flies around"? Fireflies! Give instructions on how to do the "Firefly Freeze Dance." Hand out flashlights and play "Fireflies" while the children dance around with the flashlights. When the music stops, the "fireflies" must stop and give their flashlights to the next child waiting. Continue until all children have had a turn.
11. Bring the children back to the campfire circle and sing "Twinkle, Twinkle, Little Star" with the starmaker and go to "sleep."
12. It's morning! Allow the children to use the remainder of the time for free play, allowing the children to play camping as they wish.

Additional Activities and Props

Activities

Sing: "I am Going Camping" (*Tune*: "I'm a Little Teapot")
I am going camping. (*Point to yourself.*)
Time to pack. (*Point to watch.*)
My tent, my bedroll (*Make tent with hands, then fold hands to cheek.*)
And a snack. (*Pretend to eat.*)
I'll sit by the campfire (*Pretend to warm hands.*)
Its glow so bright. (*Fan and wiggle fingers to resemble a fire.*)
Then snooze in my tent (*Pretend to sleep.*)
'Til the morning light. (*Use arms to form a sun over your head.*)

Act out: "Going on a Bear Hunt" (*Children repeat each line after you.*)
Going on a bear hunt
Going to catch a big one
I'm not afraid
What a beautiful day
Oh no!
Tall grass!
Can't go over it
Can't go under it

Guess we'll have to go through it (*Make swooshing sounds.*)

Repeat, substituting grass with a tree that you have to climb, mud that you have to slosh through, and a river that you have to swim across. On the last verse you will reach a deep dark cave and say (in a scared voice):

Can't go over it

Can't go under it

Guess we'll have to go in it

Oh. It's dark in here.

I feel something.

Lots of hair

Wet nose

Sharp teeth!

It's a bear!

Quick! Back across the river (*swim*), slosh through the mud, climb the tree, swoosh through the grass.

Good, we're home. Lock the door.

I'm never going on a bear hunt again!

Props

Tackle Box

Paint an egg carton to look like a tackle box. Write "Gone Fishin'" on the top. Make a handle out of a pipe cleaner and attach to the top (see Figure 32.2, p. 83).

Compass

Write or glue the letters N, S, E, and W on a paper plate. Cut an arrow out of construction paper and attach it to the plate with a brad. This allows the arrow to turn in different directions.

Final Thoughts

Camping is a great way to use the imagination and foster the developmental skills children need to grow and learn about the world around them. While learning about camping and other outdoor activities, children will also:

1. Use their imaginations while playing with props such as pretend campfires and nature trails to create a "camping" experience indoors.
2. Develop thinking skills as they participate in activities such as building "campfires" and tents or searching for specific animals on the "nature trail" and by using objects such as paper towel rolls, toilet paper rolls, and sheets for other purposes.
3. Enhance language skills by listening to stories and songs that use specific vocabulary words pertaining to camping and nature and by engaging in conversation about the outdoors with other children.
4. Build social skills by learning to share and converse with other children while pretending to camp, fish, look for animals, and build tents and campfires together.
5. Develop motor skills by participating in interactive songs and physical play such as pitching tents and "catching fish."

Let's Pretend: At the Train Station

Overview

Train stations can be very exciting places. Trains alone are fascinating vehicles with power, speed, and sounds. Add travelers hustling to get tickets, check luggage, and board the right train at the right time in order to get to destinations near and far

and you get a whirlwind of activity. Children love trains and they love pretending. What better way to combine the two than to set up a pretend train station? "Let's Pretend: At the Train Station" offers ideas on how to create your very own train station using props, books, music, and other train/train station-related activities.

Figure 2.1. All aboard!

Materials Needed

Props

Train: 3 or more boxes (2 big enough for a child to sit in), rope, cardboard tube, white tissue paper, paper plates

> Use a small box for the front of the train. Place the cardboard tube on top of it to make the "smokestack" and stuff the tissue paper inside the tube for "smoke." Use rope to connect the other boxes. Cut holes in the boxes for windows and doors. If you want the train to be able to "move," cut the bottom out of the boxes so that the children can walk around to make the train "run" (like a Flintstone car). Paint paper plates black and glue them to the boxes to make "wheels." Paint the train as you wish (see Figure 2.1).

Train Track: black electrical tape

> Make a train track around the room using the electrical tape. If your train is mobile, make the track wide enough for the train to fit on it (see Figure 2.2).

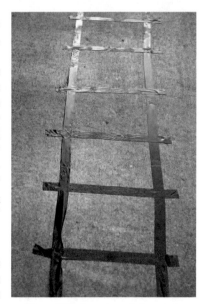

Figure 2.2. A track ready for a train

Signs: poster board or construction paper, dowels

Make railroad crossing signs and other appropriate signs on construction paper or poster board to place along the track. Attach the sign to a long dowel and use removable putty or play dough (placed on tape to protect carpeted areas) to make the sign stand.

Train Track Map: poster board

Draw a map of the room that shows where the train travels.

Train Schedule: poster board

Write out a schedule of train arrival and departure times.

Clock: paper plate, construction paper, brad

Write numbers around the edge of the plate. Make two clock hands out of construction paper and attach them to the plate using a brad.

Luggage and Tags: boxes, slips of paper, yarn

Paint various boxes to look like luggage. Use slips of paper to make tags and attach them to the luggage using yarn.

Ticket Booth: table, tissue box

Set up a table for a ticket booth. Use a tissue box as the container to drop purchased tickets into. Place the train track map, train schedule, and clock on or around the "ticket booth."

Snacks: empty food containers

Miscellaneous: engineer hat, whistle

Books

Kuklin, Susan. *All Aboard! A True Train Story*. New York: Orchard Books, 2003.

London, Jonathan. *A Train Goes Clickety-Clack*. New York: Henry Holt and Company, 2007.

Music

Allard, Peter T., and Ellen Allard. "Hello Everybody." *Sing It! Say It! Stamp It! Sway It! Volume 1* [CD]. Worcester, MA: 80-Z Music, 1999.

Coffey, James. "Down at the Station." *I Love Toy Trains—The Music* [CD]. Ft. Wayne, IN: Blue Vision Music, 2005.

At the Train Station: A Step-by-Step Program Example

1. Opening song: "Hello Everybody."
2. Train Station Talk: Talk about trains and train stations with the children. Ask questions such as:
   - What are the different types of trains? (freight, passenger, trolley, steam, subway, etc.)
   - What do trains haul? (passengers, food, animals, etc.)
   - Who drives the train?
3. Read *A Train Goes Clickety-Clack*.
4. Line up the children and have them hold on to each other to make a train. Chug around the room while listening to "Down at the Station."
5. Read *All Aboard! A True Train Story*.

6. Let's go to the train station! Tell the children to line up at the ticket booth while you give out tickets.
7. Where are we going? Study the map and train schedule. Explain to the children what both mean.
8. Check the luggage. Explain what you do with your luggage. Add tags with the child's name on it. Show them where the luggage goes.
9. All aboard! Board the train (allowing "x" number of children in each box, depending on the box size and the number of children participating).
10. Any snacks? Ask the "passengers" if they would like a snack to eat while they are traveling.
11. Lead the train around the track, stopping at signs and any other locations you have added.
12. Repeat until all children have had a turn to "ride."
13. Free play! Use the remainder of the time for free play, allowing the children to be conductors, ticket booth operators, luggage checkers, and passengers.

Additional Activities and Props

Chair Train

Arrange chairs like a passenger car. Put on an engineer hat and give each child a ticket. Pretend that you are all traveling in the train. Talk about the "scenery" as you go.

Miniature Train Station

Make a train track out of popsicle sticks and use small boxes/cartons attached with string or yarn to make a train. Use a larger box for the train station building. To add scenery, use popsicle sticks and construction paper to make signs and trees and use smaller boxes for houses, barns, or other buildings for the train to pass along the way. Follow the same activities listed in the example program.

Final Thoughts

Setting up a pretend train station is a great way to use the imagination and foster the developmental skills children need to grow and learn about the world around them. While learning about trains and train stations, children will also:

1. Use their imaginations as they explore various ways to play around the pretend train station.
2. Develop thinking skills as they consider what to do at the "train station" and where they want to "travel" and by using objects such as boxes and paper plates for various purposes.
3. Enhance language skills by listening to stories and songs that use specific vocabulary words pertaining to trains and train stations and by engaging in conversation about trains and train stations with other children.
4. Build social skills by sharing props and conversing with other children during train station play.
5. Exercise motor skills by participating in interactive songs and physical play such as working together to make the train "run."

Let's Pretend: Around Town

Overview

There is so much to see and do on a trip around town. Give children a chance to create and explore their world by setting up a make-believe town. "Let's Pretend: Around Town" offers ideas on how to introduce children to community living through books, songs, and props. Children can visit a zoo, have a bite to eat at a restaurant, browse through reading material at a library, do household chores, and so much more around this town.

Materials Needed

Props

Zoo: cardboard boxes, stuffed animals

Cut slits in the boxes to make "cages," leaving one side open with the flaps as doors (see Figure 7.1, p. 20). Place stuffed animals inside.

Restaurant: table and chairs (or place a table cloth/blanket/sheet on the floor), centerpiece of some sort, construction paper, flatware, paper plates and cups, pictures of food

Place some sort of centerpiece in the middle of the table or tablecloth on the floor (silk flowers stuck in an empty container work well). Use construction paper for placemats. Place paper plates, flatware, and paper cups on the placemats. Make a menu by folding a piece of construction paper in half and gluing pictures of food on it. Use other pictures of food for pretend dining (see Figure 3.1).

Library: books, magazines, used library cards (or make some)

Place a variety of books and magazines on a shelf or table. Use old library cards or make some out of poster board or construction paper. Create a reading area.

House: 2 boxes, bottle caps, paper towel roll, aluminum foil, cloth, empty detergent bottle, table and chairs (or place tablecloth/blanket/sheet on the

Figure 3.1. Lil' Tot Café

floor), construction paper, flatware, paper plates and cups, pictures of food, stuffed cat and/or dog with pillow or blanket

Use one box to make a stove. Cover paper plates and bottle caps with aluminum foil and use the paper plates as burners and the bottle caps as knobs (see Figure 34.1, p.

89). A small box can be used for a sink, stocked with an empty detergent bottle and a cloth to "wash dishes." Add a faucet by rolling a piece of aluminum foil and curving it at the end. Glue it to the sink box (see Figure 34.2, p. 89). Set the table with construction paper placemats, paper plates and cups, flatware, centerpiece, and pictures of food for pretend eating. Add a sleeping cat and/or dog on a blanket and/or pillow as a finishing touch for this cozy home.

Doctor's Office: table, white sheet, strips of white scrap paper, dolls, x-ray pictures, bottle caps, yarn, toilet paper rolls, popsicle sticks, bag, height chart, eye chart, straws

Cover a table with a white sheet (or place it on the floor) to make an examining table. Cut strips of white scrap paper to use as bandages. Make a stethoscope by attaching two ends of yarn to a bottle cap (like a necklace) (see Figure 28.1, p. 75). Make casts by cutting a slit down a toilet paper roll and write/draw on it as you would decorate a real cast (see Figure 28.2, p. 75). Make thermometers by cutting drinking straws in half and marking black lines and numbers along the sides. Use popsicle sticks as tongue depressors. Place these "medical supplies" in the doctor's bag. Hang an eye chart, height chart, and X-ray images (printed from the computer or drawn on paper) on the wall.

Grocery Store: empty food containers and/or saved grocery item labels and small boxes, shoe box, play money or green and gray construction paper, grocery bags, and baskets

Place empty food containers and/or small boxes with glued labels on tables or shelves. Use play money or cut up green and gray construction paper for bills and coins. Use grocery bags and/or baskets to shop.

City Bus: large box, paper plates

Use a large box to make a bus. Cut out windows and a door. Paint paper plates black and glue them to the bus for wheels. Paint the bus as you wish. If you want your bus to be mobile, cut the bottom out so that the children can walk around the room with it as they "drive" (see Figure 3.2).

Figure 3.2. Let's ride around town!

Cars: boxes, paper plates (or use ride-ons)

Make cars out of boxes. Paint them as you wish and use paper plates painted black for wheels. Use actual ride-on cars if you have them.

Roads/Parking Lot: white and yellow electrical tape

Tape electrical tape to the floor to make roads and parking lots.

Traffic Lights: milk cartons, dowels, putty/play dough

Paint milk cartons to look like traffic lights. Make them stand by attaching each carton to a dowel stuck in putty or play dough (placed on paper to protect carpeted areas).

Road Signs: poster board or construction paper, dowels, putty/play dough

Draw various road signs on construction paper or poster board. Make them stand by attaching each sign to a dowel stuck in putty or play dough (placed on paper to protect carpeted areas).

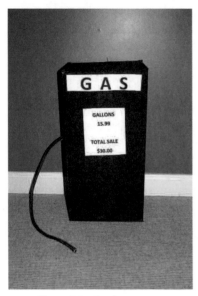

Figure 3.3. Gas for your car

Gas Pump: box, rope
Paint a box to look like a gas pump. Attach a rope to the side to use as a hose (see Figure 3.3).

Books

Carluccio, Maria. *The Sounds Around Town*. Cambridge, MA: Barefoot Books, 2008.

Hall, Kristen. *My New Town*. New York: Children's Press, 2005.

Music

Allard, Peter T., and Ellen Allard. "Hello Everybody." *Sing It! Say It! Stamp It! Sway It! Volume 1* [CD]. Worcester, MA: 80-Z Music, 1999.

Buck, Dennis. "Car Car Song." *Car Songs* [CD]. Long Branch, NJ: Kimbo Educational, 1990.

Other

"The Wheels on the Bus"

Around Town: A Step-by-Step Program Example

1. Opening song: "Hello Everybody."
2. Community Talk: Talk with the children about community living and what is in a town or city. Ask them questions such as:
   • What do you see around town? (shops, people, cars, etc.)
   • What ways can you travel around town? (cars, bus, walk, etc.)
   • Who works around town? (police, librarians, bus drivers, etc.)
3. Read *My New Town*.
4. Sing "Car Car Song."
5. Read *The Sounds Around Town*.
6. Sing "The Wheels on the Bus."
7. Let's take a trip around town! Take the children on a tour of the "town," stopping to "play" at each location.
8. Show them the bus and car routes, going over traffic safety as you do so.
9. Free play! Leave the remainder of the time open to play, allowing the children to "work" and "visit" each location as he/she chooses.

Additional Activities and Props

Miniature Town

Make a miniature town with small boxes and cartons for buildings, popsicle sticks, and construction paper for signs and trees, and smaller pieces of duct tape for roads and parking lots. Use toy cars and buses or tiny boxes to drive around the town.

Final Thoughts

Creating a make-believe town offers children numerous ways to use their imaginations and foster the developmental skills they need to grow and learn about the world around them. While learning about community living, children will also:

1. Use their imaginations to explore ways to participate in various community roles while using various props created out of household items and items that missed the garbage and by engaging in conversation.
2. Develop thinking skills as they consider appropriate play for each "location" and by using boxes, toilet paper rolls, and milk cartons for other purposes.
3. Enhance language skills by listening to stories and songs that use specific vocabulary words pertaining to towns/cities and by conversing with other children about community living.
4. Build social skills by sharing and interacting with other children through community living role-play.
5. Exercise motor skills by participating in interactive songs and physical play through various pretend play roles.

Let's Pretend: Winter Wonderland

Overview

Stuck inside on a cold winter day? Need a break from the summer heat? Create a winter wonderland! You do not need real snow or even need to be outside to enjoy winter activities. "Let's Pretend: Winter Wonderland" offers ideas on how to have lots of snowy fun with books, songs, props, and winter-related activities.

Materials Needed

Props

Figure 4.1. Snowshoes for a walk in the snow

Snowflakes: white paper, glitter
Fold and cut white paper to make various snowflake shapes. Add glitter to make them sparkle.
Igloo: egg cartons or milk jugs
Glue egg cartons together and paint white (if needed) or glue milk jugs together in a circular or square shape, layered to desired height.
Snowshoes: cardboard, string/yarn or rubber band
Cut cardboard into large ovals (about twice the size of a preschooler's foot) and attach string/yarn or rubber band around the cardboard to hold the "snowshoe" onto the child's shoe (see Figure 4.1).
Ice Skates: cardboard, wax paper, string/yarn or rubber band
Cut cardboard to a size slightly bigger than a preschooler's shoe and glue wax paper to it. Attach string/yarn or rubber band around the cardboard to hold the "skate" on to the child's shoe.
Sled: cardboard (large enough for a child to sit on), rope
Cut cardboard into a rectangular shape and make two rope handles to attach to the sides. Attach another piece of rope to the front for pulling the sled (see Figure 4.2).
Snowman: 3 white garbage bags, newspaper, two dowels, scarf, hat, mittens, black and orange construction paper
Stuff all three garbage bags with newspaper, making a large, medium, and small ball of each bag. Stack them on top of each other. Add the dowels for arms. Cut two black "coal" eyes and a "carrot" nose out of black and orange construction paper. Decorate the snowman with the scarf, hat, and mittens.

Books

Carr, Jan. *Frozen Noses*. New York: Holiday House, 1999.

Van Laan, Nancy. *When Winter Comes*. New York: Atheneum Books for Young Readers, 2000.

Music

Allard, Peter T., and Ellen Allard. "Hello Everybody." *Sing It! Say It! Stamp It! Sway It! Volume 1* [CD]. Worcester, MA: 80-Z Music, 1999.

Hammett, Carol. "Snow Fun." *Preschool Action Time* [CD]. Long Branch, NJ: Kimbo Educational, 1988.

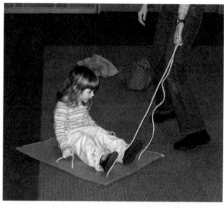

Figure 4.2. Let's go sledding!

"Snowflakes Falling from the Sky." *Piggyback Songs: Singable Songs Set to Favorite Tunes* [CD]. Long Branch, NJ: Kimbo Educational, 1995.

Other

"The Snowman" by Bev Qualheim

I looked out my window And what did I see? Snowflakes falling All around me!	I scooped up an armful, Then made a big ball, And then made another And piled them up tall.
I dressed in my warm clothes And ran out to see What I could make With the snow around me.	And what did I make? Please guess if you can. You're right if you said, "A great big snowman."

—Used by permission of Beverly A. Qualheim
www.bevscountrycottage.com

Winter Wonderland: A Step-by-Step Program Example

1. Opening song: "Hello Everybody."
2. Recite "The Snowman."
3. Winter Talk: Talk about winter with the children. Ask them questions such as:
   - What is winter? (cold season, name the months, etc.)
   - What happens in winter? (gets cold, snows, etc.)
   - What do you do in the winter? (build snowmen, ice skate, drink hot cocoa, etc.)
4. Read *When Winter Comes*.
5. Sing "Snow Fun."
6. Read *Frozen Noses*.
7. Sing "Snowflakes Falling from the Sky." Sprinkle snowflakes around the room as the music plays, allowing them to land on the children.
8. Let's pretend to be snowmen! Form a blanket of snow by lying on the floor. Roll into a snowball to become a snowman. We're now frozen. Stand very stiff/still. As the day warms, you begin to thaw. Move each body part slightly, working

from head to toe or vice versa. Now we can play! Let's dance and skate. Oh no, we're melting! Get smaller and weaker as you sink to the floor.

9. Let's build a snowman! Use three newspaper-stuffed white garbage bags for the body. Add dowels for stick arms. Dress the snowman with eyes, nose, scarf, hat, and mittens.
10. Time for a snowshoe walk! Give each child a pair of "snowshoes" and pretend to walk in a snowy forest.
11. Who wants to ice skate? Give each child a pair of "ice skates" and lead the child to an imaginary pond. Pretend to skate.
12. Let's go sledding! Give each child a turn to ride on the "sled" as you pull.
13. Free play! Use the remainder of the time for free play, allowing the children to play in the igloo, build snowmen, go on snowshoe walks, ice skate, and sled as they choose.

Additional Activities and Props

Activities

Sing: "I'm a Little Snowman" (*Tune*: I'm a Little Teapot)
I'm a little snowman short and fat.
Here are my buttons and here is my hat.
When the sun comes out, I cannot play.
I just slowly melt away.

Props

Flannel Board Snowman
Use felt to make a snowman's body, eyes, nose, mouth, and clothing.

Sock Snowman
Fill a sock with rice, making three separate sections to form the body. Add eyes, nose, mouth and arms.

Fake Snow
Spread white stuffing, shredded scrap paper, or foam peanuts around the room.

Final Thoughts

Creating a winter wonderland indoors generates a lot of opportunity for imaginative play and fosters the developmental skills children need to learn about the world around them. While learning about winter and the activities that can be enjoyed during the winter season, children will also:

1. Use their imaginations to engage in pretend winter play by using props such as "igloos," "ice skates," "snow shoes," "sleds," and "snow."
2. Develop thinking skills as they participate in activities such as "building snowmen" and by using items such as egg cartons/jugs, trash bags, and cardboard pieces for other purposes.
3. Enhance language skills by listening to stories and songs that use specific vocabulary words pertaining to winter and by communicating with others during make-believe winter play.
4. Build social skills by sharing props with others and by engaging in winter play.
5. Exercise motor skills by participating in interactive songs and physical play such as "skating" and "sledding."

Let's Pretend: In a Parade

Overview

Floats, music, costumes! Parades are lots of fun to watch and participate in. "Let's Pretend: In a Parade" offers ideas on how to create a make-believe parade complete with "floats," music, and marching by using books, songs, props, and parade-related activities.

Materials Needed

Props

Paper Plate Shaker: 2 paper plates, rice/dried beans
> Attach two paper plates together and add rice or beans before closing completely.

Drum: empty plastic or cardboard container with lid (yogurt tub, ice cream pail, oatmeal container)
> Attach yarn or string to the sides of the container so that it can be hung around the neck (see Figure 5.1).

String Instruments: empty container or shoebox, rubber bands
> Stretch several rubber bands around the container or shoe box so that they cross over the opening (see Figure 5.2).

Can Shaker: aluminum can, rice/dried beans
> Put rice or beans inside of an empty aluminum can and place tape over the opening.

Cymbals: pot lids

Paper Plate Tambourine: paper plate, pipe cleaners, buttons
> Punch holes around the edge of the paper plate. String several buttons onto pipe cleaners and loop the pipe cleaners through the holes, adjusting the length accordingly.

Rhythm Sticks: wooden and/or metal spoons

Float: box (big enough for child and/or stuffed animals) or wagon, construction paper, streamers, confetti, balloons, rope
> Decorate a box to look like a float. Punch a hole in the front to attach a rope for pulling.

Miscellaneous: streamers, balloons, confetti

Figure 5.1. Beat the drum!

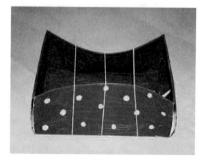

Figure 5.2. Let's make music!

Books

Crews, Donald. *Parade*. New York: Greenwillow Books, 1983.

Murphy, Stuart J. *Spunky Monkeys on Parade*. New York: Harper Collins Publishers, 1999.

Music

Allard, Peter T., and Ellen Allard. "Hello Everybody." *Sing It! Say It! Stamp It! Sway It! Volume 1* [CD]. Worcester, MA: 80-Z Music, 1999.

Cohen, Penny. "Marching Band Practice." *Hop n Bop Songs for You and Me* [CD]. San Diego, CA: Children's Creative Programming Partnership, 2008.

Palmer, Hap. "Main Street Parade." *Modern Tunes for Rhythms and Instruments* [CD]. Freeport, NY: Activity Records, 2004.

Palmer, Hap. "Parade of Colors." *Hap Palmer's Can a Cherry Pie Wave Goodbye?* [CD]. Topanga, CA: Hap-Pal Music, 1993.

In a Parade: A Step-by-Step Program Example

1. Opening song: "Hello Everybody."
2. Parade Talk: Talk about parades with the children. Ask them questions such as:
   - When do we have parades? (holidays, festivals, etc.)
   - What do you see in parades? (floats, marching bands, clowns, etc.)
3. Read *Parade*.
4. Pass out colored streamers or construction paper and use while listening to "Parade of Colors."
5. Read *Spunky Monkeys on Parade*.
6. Time for marching band practice! Listen to "Marching Band Practice" to warm up for the "real parade."
7. Parade time! Let the children choose props to use for the parade (instruments, floats, streamers, etc.). Then, line them all up and play "Main Street Parade" as you all parade around the room.
8. Free Play! Use the remainder of the time for free play, allowing the children to create their own parade.

Final Thoughts

Pretending to have a parade is a fun way to use the imagination and foster the developmental skills children need to grow and discover the world around them. While learning about parades and what a parade consists of, children also:

1. Use their imaginations to engage in pretend play by using various objects as instruments, floats, and other parade paraphernalia.
2. Develop thinking skills as they make music and consider how to be in a "parade" and by using objects such as paper plates, empty containers, and kitchen items for various purposes.
3. Enhance language skills as they hear stories and songs that use specific vocabulary words about parades and by conversing with others during parade play.
4. Build social skills by learning to share parade props and by engaging in conversation during play.
5. Exercise motor skills by participating in interactive songs and physical play such as parade marching.

Let's Pretend: A Spring Picnic

Overview

The flowers are blooming. The birds are singing. It's spring! Wouldn't it be nice to have a picnic? Grab a basket, some food, and a kite. "Let's Pretend: A Spring Picnic" offers ideas on how to set up a spring picnic indoors.

Figure 6.1. Ready to grill!

Materials Needed

Props

Food: printed pictures or construction paper, empty food containers

> Print pictures of bread, fruit, fish, hot dogs, etc., or draw food on construction paper. Save empty food containers (ketchup bottles, yogurt containers, snack boxes) and use for additional props.

Basket
Paper Plates
Cups
Utensils: flatware and grilling (spatula and other nonsharp utensils)
Fire: real wood or paper towel rolls, red, yellow, and orange tissue paper

> Arrange firewood or paper towel rolls as you would when building a real fire. Stuff the tissue paper in the "wood" for "flames" (see Figure 6.1).

Grill: baking rack

> Place the rack over the "fire" to use as a grill.

Blanket
Kites: construction paper, yarn

> Draw diamond shapes on construction paper and attach a piece of yarn to the bottom. Decorate as you desire (see Figure 6.2).

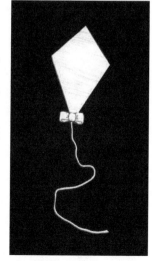

Figure 6.2. Let's go fly a kite!

Bubbles

Spring Decorations: construction paper, printed pictures

Draw or print flowers, insects, and trees and display them throughout the picnic area.

Books

Alborough, Jez. *It's the Bear*. Cambridge, MA: Candlewick Press, 1991.

Hamilton, Richard. *Polly's Picnic*. New York: Bloomsbury, 2003.

Music

Allard, Peter T., and Ellen Allard. "Hello Everybody." *Sing It! Say It! Stamp It! Sway It! Volume 1* [CD]. Worcester, MA: 80-Z Music, 1999.

"My Kite." *Piggyback Songs: Singable Poems Set to Favorite Tunes* [CD]. Long Branch, NJ: Kimbo Educational, 1995.

Raffi. "Going on a Picnic." *Corner Grocery Store* [CD]. Cambridge, MA: Rounder Records, 1979.

A Spring Picnic: A Step-by-Step Program Example

1. Opening song: "Hello Everybody."
2. Talk about picnics with the children. Ask them questions such as:
   - What is a picnic?
   - What do you eat on a picnic? (sandwiches, grilled food, fruit, lemonade, etc.)
   - What other activities can you do on a picnic? (fly a kite, make cloud pictures, blow bubbles, play games, etc.)
   - What do you do when you are finished with your picnic? (clean up the trash)
   - What do you see on a picnic? (flowers, trees, insects, etc.)
3. Read *Polly's Picnic*.
4. Pass out printed food items mentioned in "Going on a Picnic." While listening to the song, have the children hold up the appropriate food.
5. Read *It's the Bear*.
6. Let's prepare for our picnic! Pass out the food items and pack the picnic basket(s). If there are not enough baskets for each child, let each child put an item in one shared basket.
7. Let's go! Place a blanket on the floor with the basket. Build the "fire" and place the "grill" on top.
8. Grilling time! Give each child something to grill (hot dog, fish, hamburger, etc.).
9. Time to eat! Now that the picnic is set up and the food is grilled gather everyone onto the blanket. Pass out plates and cups and allow the children to pick out the "food" from the basket.
10. Don't litter! Talk to the children about the importance of picking up the trash.
11. Let's fly a kite! Give each child a premade kite, or allow them to make one. Listen to "My Kite" as they "fly" their kites around the room.
12. Bubbles! Let everyone have a chance to play/blow bubbles.
13. Free play! Use the remainder of the time for free play, allowing the children to play picnic as they wish.

Final Thoughts

As eating and pretending often go hand in hand, setting up a picnic is an ideal way to use the imagination and foster the developmental skills children need to grow and learn about the world around them. While pretending to be on a picnic, children also:

1. Use their imaginations as they play with props to create a picnic experience.
2. Develop thinking skills as they participate in activities such as identifying food and building a "fire" and by using objects such as empty food containers and paper towel rolls for other purposes.
3. Enhance language skills as they listen to stories and songs about picnics and converse with other children during picnic play.
4. Build social skills as they share the picnic props and engage in conversation during play.
5. Exercise motor skills as they participate in interactive songs and physical play such as "kite-flying."

Let's Pretend: At the Animal Hospital

Overview

Children love to take on various roles while playing. This type of play makes excellent use of the imagination and helps develop so many other skills as well. Pretending to be an animal doctor is one of many roles children can imagine themselves to be in during play. "Let's Pretend: At the Animal Hospital" offers ideas on how to set up a make-believe animal hospital using books, songs, props and animal hospital-related activities.

Materials Needed

Props

Figure 7.1. A cozy kennel

Figure 7.2. A cast to heal a puppy

Kennels: box(es)
> Cut slits in the boxes to make "cage-like kennels," leaving one side open with the flaps as doors. Place stuffed animals inside (see Figure 7.1).

X-rays: construction paper or pictures
> Print X-ray pictures from the computer or draw some on construction paper.

Casts: toilet paper roll
> Cut a slit down a toilet paper roll and write/draw on it as you would decorate a real cast (see Figure 7.2).

Syringe (without needle): available at pharmacies

Thermometer: drinking straw
> Make thermometers by cutting drinking straws in half and marking black lines and numbers along the sides.

Stuffed Animals

Bandages: scrap paper, tape
> Cut scrap paper into strips and use tape to apply to stuffed animals.

Stethoscope: bottle cap, yarn/string
> Make a stethoscope by attaching two ends of yarn to a bottle cap (like a necklace) (see Figure 28.1, p. 75).

Doctor's Bag
Dog Biscuits: cardboard
Cut up pieces of cardboard to make dog biscuits.
Sink: box, aluminum foil, empty bottle
A small box can be used for a sink, stocked with an empty bottle of "dog shampoo" to bathe them. Add a faucet by rolling a piece of aluminum foil and curving it at the end. Glue it to the sink box (see Figure 27.2, p. 73).
Brush
Barn: box
Use a cardboard box as a barn, decorating as you wish.

Books

Feiffer, Jules. *Bark, George*. New York: HarperCollins Publishers, 1999.
Huneck, Stephen. *Sally Goes to the Vet*. New York: Harry N. Abrams, Inc., 2004.

Music

Allard, Peter T., and Ellen Allard. "Hello Everybody." *Sing It! Say It! Stamp It! Sway It! Volume 1* [CD]. Worcester, MA: 80-Z Music, 1999.

Other

"Old MacDonald"

At the Animal Hospital: A Step-by-Step Program Example

1. Opening song: "Hello Everybody."
2. Talk about animal hospitals/veterinaries with the children. Ask them questions such as:
   - What is an animal hospital/veterinary?
   - Why do animals go there? (sick, hurt, shots, boarding, grooming, etc.)
   - Who takes care of them? (veterinarian, assistants, etc.)
   - Where do you find animal hospitals? (town or country)
3. Read *Sally Goes to the Vet*.
4. Pass out appropriate stuffed animals or picture of animals and sing "Old MacDonald." Ask the children to hold up the animal they have been given at the appropriate time during the song.
5. Read *Bark, George*.
6. Let's visit the animal hospital! If the children used stuffed animals during the "Old MacDonald" song, let them bring them to the "vet" for a check.
7. Who's staying overnight? "Check in" the animals that will be staying overnight. Put them in the kennels.
8. Are there any hurt animals? Take the "hurt" or "sick" ones to the table. Take their temperature, give them medicine, put a cast on them, etc. Show the children what each prop is for and explain what you are doing to make the animals "feel better."
9. Grooming time! "Bathe" and "brush" the animals there for grooming.

10. Let's visit the farm. Explain that sometimes vets have to go to farms to take care of animals such as horses. Grab the doctor's bag and take them to the farm area to care for the animals there.
11. Free play! Use the remainder of the time for free play, allowing the children to play in the animal hospital area as they wish.

Final Thoughts

Pretending to be a veterinarian and setting up a make-believe animal hospital is a great way for children to use their imaginations to try on a different role and to foster the developmental skills they need to grow and learn about the world around them. While learning about animal hospitals and what veterinarians do, children also:

1. Use their imaginations as they use props to engage in animal hospital play.
2. Develop thinking skills as they consider a veterinarian's job and what they need to do to care for animals and by using items such as boxes, toilet paper rolls, and drinking straws for other purposes.
3. Enhance language skills as they listen to stories and songs/music about animal hospitals and engage in conversation during play.
4. Build social skills as they share props and talk with other children about the animal hospital.
5. Exercise motor skills by participating in interactive songs and through physical play.

Let's Pretend: A Day at the Beach

Overview

The sand. The sun. The waves. Who doesn't enjoy a trip to the beach? Even if you don't live near the coast (or maybe you do but want to avoid the crowd) you can have a day at the beach without stepping outside. "Let's Pretend: A Day at the Beach" offers ideas on how to set up a make-believe beach complete with sand, an ocean, and lots of beachy fun with books, songs, props and beach-related activities.

Materials Needed

Props

Ocean: blue tarp, butcher paper, or blue cellophane
> Use walls or furniture to hang blue tarp or butcher paper in a way that children can play under it (as if being under water).

Sand: brown or white blankets/sheets, cardboard, or butcher paper
> Spread brown or white blankets/sheets, cardboard, or butcher paper under the "ocean" and also extend it beyond the ocean to create a "beach."

Sea Shells: printed pictures or real shells
> Print seashell pictures from the computer or use real shells. Place around the "beach" and at the "bottom of the ocean."

Sea Creatures: printed pictures
> Print pictures of sea creatures (crabs, fish, etc.) and place in the "ocean" and along the "beach."

Limbo Stick: broom handle, rope, or a long stick

Buckets: paper cups, pipe cleaners
> Use a cup for the bucket and attach a pipe cleaner for a handle (see Figure 8.1).

Sandcastle: boxes, sandpaper
> Glue sandpaper to various boxes. Leave the boxes separated so that the children can stack them to build "sandcastles" (see Figure 8.2).

Miscellaneous: sunshades, empty suntan lotion bottles, towels, beach balls, floats, lounge chairs

Figure 8.1. A sand bucket

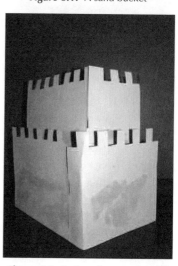

Figure 8.2. Let's make a sandcastle!

Books

Roosa, Karen. *Beach Day*. New York: Clarion Books, 2001.

Schertle, Alice. 2004. *All You Need for a Beach*. San Diego: Silver Whistle/Harcourt, Inc.

Music

Allard, Peter T., and Ellen Allard. "Hello Everybody." *Sing It! Say It! Stamp It! Sway It! Volume 1* [CD]. Worcester, MA: 80-Z Music, 1999.

Wiggles. "Having Fun at the Beach." *Wake Up, Jeff!* [CD]. New York: Lyrick Studios, 2000.

A Day at the Beach: A Step-by-Step Program Example

1. Opening song: "Hello Everybody."
2. Talk to the children about the beach and ocean. Ask them questions such as:
   - What can you do at the beach? (swim, build sandcastles, etc.)
   - How do you protect yourself from getting burned by the sun? (wear sunscreen, play under an umbrella, etc.)
3. Read *All You Need for a Beach*.
4. Listen/dance to "Having Fun at the Beach."
5. Read *Beach Day*.
6. Time for beach limbo! Play beachy music as the children go under the limbo stick as various sea creatures (swim like a fish, crawl like a crab, etc.).
7. Let's find shells. Give the children "buckets" and take them on a walk along the "beach" to look for shells.
8. Let's play in the waves! Stand at the edge of the "ocean" and pretend to run from the waves and jump into the waves.
9. Time to swim! Show the children how to "swim" and then take them out into the "ocean." Then take them "under water" and show them various sea creatures.
10. Free play! Use the remainder of the time for free play, allowing the children to play at the "beach" as they choose.

Additional Props

Jellyfish
Blow up balloons and attach streamers to them.

Clams
Attach two pie plates together and stuff with cotton balls (see Figure 17.1, p. 47).

Treasure Chest
Paint a box to look like a treasure chest and place at the bottom of the "ocean."

Submarine
Use a box big enough for one or more children to get in. Paint and decorate it to look like a submarine.

Final Thoughts

Having a make-believe day at the beach is a great way to use the imagination and foster the developmental skills children need to grow and learn about the world around them. While learning about the beach and ocean, children also learn to:

1. Use their imaginations to explore ways to play at the beach by using props and engaging in conversation.
2. Develop thinking skills as they participate in beach activities and by using objects such as paper cups, boxes, and sheets/blankets for other purposes.
3. Enhance language skills as they listen to stories and songs about the beach and by conversing with other children during beach play.
4. Build social skills by sharing props and talking with other children during play.
5. Exercise motor skills by participating in interactive songs and physical play such as pretend swimming and building sandcastles.

Let's Pretend: On the Farm

Overview

Farms are full of life and activity. Not only are there lots of animals to see, feed, and care for but there are tractors to ride, gardens to pick, and scarecrows to make. "Let's Pretend: On the Farm" provides ideas on how to introduce children to life on a farm using books, songs, props and farm-related activities.

Materials Needed

Props

Barn: box
Use a large box for a barn. Paint and decorate it as you wish.

Hay Bales: boxes, straw
Glue straw to the boxes to create hay bales.

Bandanas

Straw Hats

Scarecrow: newspaper, pants, shirt, boots, hat, pillowcase
Stuff the pants, shirt, and pillowcase with newspaper. Tie the pillowcase and tuck it into the neck of the shirt. Tuck the shirt into the pants. Place the boots over the pants leg. Draw a face on the pillowcase and add a hat (see Figure 21.1, p. 58).

Stuffed Animals

Animal Puppets or Pictures

Trough: box
Use a box as a trough to feed the animals.

Fence: cardboard, paint
Cut a piece of cardboard to look like a fence. Create a fold on both ends to make it stand. Paint it as desired (see Figure 9.1).

Figure 9.1. A place for your horse

Horses: broomsticks, printed horse head pictures
Print horse head pictures (2 matching ones for each horse) and tape to the broom.

Tractor: box (big enough for a child to sit in), paper plates
Paint a box green to make a tractor (you can decorate it to make it as elaborate as you want). Paint paper plates black and use for tires.

Cow: poster board, latex gloves

Draw a cow on poster board and cut it out. Attach latex gloves to the belly for udders. You can also poke a tiny hole on each fingertip and fill the gloves with water to create a more realistic milking experience (see Figure 9.2).

Garden: green Styrofoam, printed pictures of flowers and vegetables, dowels

Print pictures of vegetables (roots are best, such as carrots) and flowers and tape to dowels. Stick the flowers and vegetables into the Styrofoam (see Figure 22.1, p. 60).

Basket

Eggs: purchase plastic eggs or cut white ovals out of construction paper

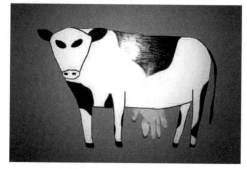

Figure 9.2. Let's milk a cow!

Books

Kutner, Merrily. *Down on the Farm*. New York: Holiday House, 2004.
Ransom, Candice. *Tractor Day*. New York: Walker and Company, 2007.

Music

Allard, Peter T., and Ellen Allard. "Hello Everybody." *Sing It! Say It! Stamp It! Sway It! Volume 1* [CD]. Worcester, MA: 80-Z Music, 1999.

Other

"Old MacDonald"

On the Farm: A Step-by-Step Program Example

1. Opening song: "Hello Everybody."
2. Talk about farms with the children. Ask them questions such as:
   - What animals do you see on a farm and what sounds do they make? (cows, horses, chickens, etc.)
   - What crops are grown on farms? (corn, beans, etc.)
   - What activities take place on farms? (milking cows, picking gardens, gathering eggs, etc.)
   - What are some things you would find on a farm? (tractor, animals, barn, etc.)
3. Read *Down on the Farm*.
4. Sing "Old MacDonald." Use puppets or pictures for each animal or give each child an animal picture and tell the child to hold up the animal as it is called out in the song.
5. Read *Tractor Day*.
6. Let's go to the farm! Pretend to drive a tractor. Bump up and down in your seat as you "drive."
7. We're here. Let's feed the animals. Let the children put the "hay bales" in the "troughs."
8. Time to pick the garden! Let the children fill baskets with flowers and vegetables from the garden.

9. Let's gather the eggs. Bring the children over to the barn where the eggs are (or you can scatter them around the farm area and let them hunt for the eggs) and let them fill their baskets with eggs.
10. Let's make a scarecrow. Work together to stuff the clothes. Then add the hat and boots.
11. Time to milk the cow! Show the children how a cow is milked and then let them take turns.
12. Free play! Use the remainder of the time for free play, allowing the children to play on the "farm" as they wish.

Additional Props

Barn

If you don't have a box for a barn you can create a barn area by drawing a barn on red butcher paper, cutting it out, and taping it to the wall.

Garden (an alternative to the one described in the previous Props section)

Make a wall garden by taping brown paper (dirt) to the wall and then taping pictures of vegetables to the "dirt." Children can pick the vegetables from the wall. The tape will last longer if the garden pieces are laminated.

Final Thoughts

A make-believe farm offers many ways for children to use their imaginations and foster the developmental skills they need to grow and learn about the world around them. While learning about life on a farm, children will also:

1. Use their imaginations to discover ways to "work" around a farm by using props made from various objects such as boxes, felt, and broomsticks and by conversing with others during play.
2. Develop thinking skills as they participate in various farm-related activities and by using objects such as boxes and Styrofoam for other purposes.
3. Enhance language skills as they listen to stories and songs that use specific vocabulary words pertaining to farms and by engaging in farm-play conversations.
4. Build social skills by learning to share props and conversing during play.
5. Exercise motor skills as they participate in interactive songs and physical play such as "feeding" the "animals," "milking the cow," and "picking the garden."

Let's Pretend: Firefighters

Overview

Hurry! Hurry! Firefighters to the rescue. Pretending to be a firefighter opens up a great opportunity for role-play. "Let's Pretend: Firefighters" offers ideas on how to introduce children to the occupation of firefighters using books, music, props and firefighter-related activities.

Materials Needed

Props

Fire Truck: red bedsheet, paper plates
Cut the shape of a fire truck out of a red bedsheet. Paint paper plates black and use as wheels. Use a black marker to draw a ladder. Make several rows of chairs and tape the bedsheet to one side (see Figure 10.1).

Firefighter Hat: purchased or cut one out of construction paper

Badge: construction paper
Draw badges and cut them out of construction paper.

Stuffed Dalmatian

Water Hose: jump rope

Burning House: box, construction paper
Paint a box to look like a house. Add orange and yellow "flames" to the sides using construction paper (see Figure 10.2).

Figure 10.1. Firefighters to the rescue!

Books

Desimini, Lisa. *Dot, the Fire Dog.* New York: Blue Sky Press, 2001.

Hamilton, Kersten. *Firefighters to the Rescue.* New York: Viking, 2005.

Music

Allard, Peter T., and Ellen Allard. "Hello Everybody." *Sing It! Say It! Stamp It! Sway It! Volume 1* [CD]. Worcester, MA: 80-Z Music, 1999.

Figure 10.2. The house is on fire!

"Hurry, Hurry, Drive the Fire Truck." *Barney's Favorites Volume 1* [CD]. NewYork: SBK Records, 1993.

Firefighters: A Step-by-Step Program Example

1. Opening song: "Hello Everybody."
2. Talk to the children about firefighters and fire safety. Ask them questions such as:
   - What do firefighters do? (rescue people, put out fires, etc.)
   - How do you stay safe from fires? (don't play with matches, turn things off, etc.)
3. Practice stop, drop, and roll.
4. Read *Firefighters to the Rescue.*
5. Listen to "Hurry, Hurry, Drive the Fire Truck."
6. Read *Dot, the Fire Dog.*
7. Firefighter training time! Lead the children through a "mini workout" (jumping jacks, running in place, etc.). Then give them their gear (hat and badge) to make them "official" firefighters.
8. The phone rings...emergency! Let's go put out a fire! Tell everyone to get in the fire truck and pretend to drive to the burning house.
9. The house needs water! Let all the children take turns using the "hose" to put out the "fire."
10. Free play! Use the remainder of the time for free play, allowing the children to play firefighters as they wish.

Final Thoughts

Firefighter role-playing opens a lot of room for imaginative play and fosters the developmental skills children need to grow and learn about the world around them. While learning about firefighters, children will also:

1. Use their imaginations while playing with props such as pretend water hoses and fire trucks to create a firefighter experience.
2. Develop thinking skills as they learn about fire safety and use objects such as boxes and jump ropes for other purposes.
3. Enhance language skills as they listen to stories and music and converse with other children about firefighters.
4. Build social skills as they share props and engage in conversation during play.
5. Exercise motor skills as they participate in interactive songs and physical activities such as "training to be a firefighter."

Let's Pretend: At the Zoo

Overview

Zoos are places to learn about animals and their habitats. Not only do visitors and staff get to see the animals up-close but they also get to feed and pet many. "Let's Pretend: At the Zoo" offers ways to introduce children to animals and zoo life using books, songs, props, and zoo-related activities.

Materials Used

Props

Tickets: paper
> Use scrap paper for tickets.

Welcome Gate: 2 tables, sign
> Place two tables side-by-side, with just enough room to walk between the two. Decorate the tables to look like the entrance to a zoo, complete with a sign.

Ticket Box: box
> Use a box (tissue box works well) to drop tickets into. Place at the entrance.

Cages: boxes
> Cut slits in the boxes to make "cages," leaving one side open with the flaps as doors. Place stuffed animals inside (see Figure 7.1, p. 20).

Pond: blue poster board or butcher paper, construction paper
> Cut a large piece out of blue poster board or butcher paper shaped like a pond (see Figure 1.2, p. 1).

Aquatic Animals: construction paper or printed pictures
> Draw pictures of aquatic animals on construction paper and cut out. You can also print pictures from your computer. Place the pictures in the "pond."

Food: scrap paper
> Shred scrap paper to use as animal food.

Bird Cage: box(es), dowel, bird puppet or picture
> Cut slits in box(es) to make "cage(s)," leaving one side open with the flaps as doors. Stick a dowel in putty to stand in the cage(s) (see Figure 11.1). Place the bird on the dowel.

Figure 11.1. A cozy home for a bird

Aquarium: box, blue cellophane, fish pictures (construction paper or printed), white or clear string

Remove the flaps from one side of a box. Tape and/or hang fish inside the box. Stretch blue cellophane across the opening of the box.

Binoculars: 2 toilet paper rolls, yarn

Attach yarn to two toilet paper rolls by punching a hole in each roll and making a knot in the yarn to keep it from sliding through the hole (see Figure 16.3, p. 46).

Vet Clinic: table, X-ray pictures printed from the computer, toilet paper rolls, drinking straw, table, bottle cap, yarn/string

Place X-ray pictures in the table area. Make casts out of toilet paper rolls by cutting a slit down the roll (see Figure 7.2, p. 20). Make a thermometer out of a straw by cutting the straw in half and marking black lines and numbers down the side. Make a stethoscope by attaching two ends of yarn to a bottle cap (like a necklace) (see Figure 28.1, p. 75).

Farm Area: red poster board or butcher paper, boxes, stuffed animals

Use poster board to create a barn on the wall or cut a barn shape out of butcher paper. Paint boxes to look like hay bales. Unfold a large box and cut out a "picket fence" (see Figure 9.1, p. 26). Place stuffed animals around the area.

Books

Ormerod, Jan. *When We Went to the Zoo*. New York: Lothrop, Lee and Sheppard Books, 1990.

Wilson, Karma. *Animal Strike at the Zoo. It's True!* New York: HarperCollins Publishers, 2006.

Music

Allard, Peter T., and Ellen Allard. "Hello Everybody." *Sing It! Say It! Stamp It! Sway It! Volume1* [CD]. Worcester, MA: 80-Z Music, 1999.

Banana Slug String Band. "Animals Are Dancing." *Penguin Parade* [CD]. Redway, CA: Music for Little People, 1996.

Raffi. "Going to the Zoo." *Singable Songs for the Very Young* [CD]. Cambridge, MA: Rounder, 1976.

At the Zoo: Step-by-Step Program Example

1. Opening song: "Hello Everybody."
2. Talk about zoo life with the children. Ask them questions such as:
   - What is a zoo?
   - What do you see at a zoo? (animals, animal homes, shows, etc.)
   - Who works there? (zookeepers, vets, etc.)
3. Read *When We Went to the Zoo*.
4. Sing/dance to "Animals Are Dancing."
5. Read *Animal Strike At the Zoo. It's True!*
6. Sing/act out "Going to the Zoo."
7. Let's visit the zoo! Pass out tickets to everyone and give them binoculars to view the animals.

8. We're at the gate. Tell everyone to drop their tickets into the ticket box as they pass through the gate.
9. Let's see the animals. Take the children on a tour of the zoo. Visit each "exhibit" and talk about the "animals." What does their home look like? What are they doing? What are they eating? Let the children feed the animals.
10. Time to take care of the sick. Take the children to the vet area and use the props to show them how to "care" for the "sick animals."
11. Free play! Use the remainder of the time as free play, allowing the children to explore the zoo as visitors and/or staff.

Final Thoughts

Pretending to visit and/or work at a zoo is a great way to use the imagination and foster the developmental skills children need to grow and learn about the world around them. While learning about zoo life, children will also:

1. Use their imaginations while playing with props such as pretend exhibits and binoculars to create a zoo-like experience.
2. Develop thinking skills as they participate in activities such as "caring" for "sick animals" and by engaging in conversation about zoo life.
3. Enhance language skills by listening to stories and songs that use specific vocabulary words pertaining to zoo life and by conversing with others during play.
4. Build social skills as they share props and converse with other children while pretending to visit and/or work at the zoo.
5. Exercise motor skills by participating in interactive songs and physical play.

Let's Pretend: Construction Workers

Overview

Constructive play is an essential form of play for children. What better way to provide constructive play than by pretending to be construction workers? "Let's Pretend: Construction Workers" offers ideas on how to use books, songs, props, and activities to introduce children to the world of construction while also providing time to think and build creations of their own.

Figure 12.1. A toolbox for construction play

Materials Needed

Props

Toolbox: shoe box
> Use a shoe box for a toolbox. Decorate as you wish (see Figure 12.1).

Tools: cardboard
> Draw saw and hammer shapes on cardboard. Cut them out and color them to look like saws and hammers.

Building Blocks: cardboard boxes
> Use various sizes of cardboard boxes for building blocks.

Rulers: rulers or carboard/construction paper
> Use real rulers or make pretend ones out of cardboard or construction paper.

Signs: poster board or construction paper
> Make "Construction Zone" and "Hard Hat Area" signs using poster board and/or construction paper.

Tool Belt: cloth
> Cut a piece of cloth big enough to go across the front of a child. Hot glue ties to each side and pockets to the front.

Miscellaneous: hard hats, yellow and black tape, play dough

Books

Carter, Don. *Get to Work Trucks*. Brookfield, CT: Roaring Brook Press, 2002.
Sobel, June. *B Is for Bulldozer*. San Diego: Harcourt, Inc., 2003.

Music

Allard, Peter T., and Ellen Allard. "Hello Everybody." *Sing It! Say It! Stamp It! Sway It! Volume 1* [CD]. Worcester, MA: 80-Z Music, 1999.

Other

"Construction Worker Song" (*Tune*: "London Bridge")

This is the way we hammer nails, hammer nails, hammer nails.
This is the way we hammer nails,
So early in the morning.

Continue with:

This is the way we drill a hole, saw the wood, turn the screw, stack the bricks, paint the walls, stir the paint, etc.

Construction Workers: Step-by-Step Program Example

1. Opening song: "Hello Everybody."
2. Talk with the children about construction work. Ask them questions such as:
   • What do construction workers build? (buildings, roads, etc.)
   • What types of tools do they use? (hammers, saws, drills, etc.)
   • What do they drive? (diggers, cement mixers, etc.)
3. Read *B Is for Bulldozer*.
4. Sing "Construction Workers Song."
5. Read *Get to Work Trucks*.
6. Let's Build! Introduce the tools and supplies provided at the "construction site." Talk about things that can be built.
7. Free play! Use the remainder of the time for free play, allowing the children to explore the materials and create as they wish.

Final Thoughts

Allowing time for children to be creative during construction play encourages them to use their imaginations and fosters the developmental skills they need to grow and learn about the world around them. While learning about construction workers, children will also:

1. Use their imaginations to construct things with the materials provided.
2. Develop thinking skills as they decide how to put things together to build.
3. Enhance language skills as they listen to stories and songs that use specific vocabulary words pertaining to construction work and by engaging in conversation during play.
4. Build social skills as they work with others to build.
5. Exercise motor skills as they participate in interactive songs and physical play such as building things.

Let's Pretend: Western Days

Overview

Horses, cowboys, ranches, gold! Round up your cattle and let's head west. "Let's Pretend: Western Days" offers ideas on how to set up a make-believe western area using books, songs, activities, and props that introduce children to life out west.

Materials Needed

Props

Campfire: real firewood or paper towel rolls; red, yellow, and orange tissue paper
Arrange firewood or paper towel rolls as you would when building a real fire. Stuff red, yellow, and orange tissue paper in the "wood" for "flames" (see Figure 1.1, p. 1).

Horses: dowels and printed horse pictures or brooms and/or printed horse pictures
Print horse head pictures (two matching ones for each horse) and tape to the dowels or brooms.

Hay Bales: boxes, straw
Glue straw to the boxes to create hay bales.

Apples: red construction paper
Make apples out of red construction paper.

Jail: box
Use a box large enough for a child to get in. Cut out a "barred window." Paint the jail black or gray.

Wanted Posters: printed pictures, construction paper
Print antique-looking pictures of people (cowboys work well) or print pictures of the children. Glue the pictures onto beige construction paper and write "Wanted" at the top (include a "for" caption under the picture for added effect). Crumple and tear edges of the poster to give it an old look (see Figure 13.1). Place near the jail.

Cows: white balloons
Blow up white balloons and color black spots on them.

Figure 13.1. Lil' Outlaw

Ranch Sign: construction paper
Create a name for your ranch and make a sign out of construction paper.

Horseshoes: cardboard
Cut horseshoe shapes out of cardboard. Hang them around the ranch area.

Cactus: green poster board

Make cactus cutouts on poster board and tape to the walls.

Trail Ride: pictures of snakes and lizards, cacti, rocks made out of crumpled newspaper painted gray and brown

Create a path to use as a trail ride. Tape cacti and other western-looking wildlife to the walls and place snakes, lizards, and rocks along the path.

Cowboy Flannel Board: flannel and flannel board

Make a cowboy and his attire out of flannel (hat, vest, boots, etc.).

Gold Panning: box, shredded paper, cardboard

Fill a box with shredded paper. Paint round cardboard pieces gold and scatter throughout the box.

Miscellaneous: saddle, empty food cans, bandanas, sheriff's hat

Books

Czernecki, Stefan. *Ride 'Em, Cowboy*. Vancouver, BC: Simply Read Books.

Rounds, Glen. *Cowboys*. New York: Holiday House,1991.

Music

Allard, Peter T., and Ellen Allard. "Hello Everybody." *Sing It! Say It! Stamp It! Sway It! Volume 1* [CD]. Worcester, MA: 80-Z Music, 1999.

Howdy, Buck. "Born to Ride." *Skidaddle* [CD]. Nashville: MCA Nashville, 2003.

Western Days: Step-by-Step Program Example

1. Opening song: "Hello Everybody."
2. Talk with the children about the Wild West (cowboys, ranches, etc.). Ask them questions such as:
   - What do cowboys do? (ride horses, round up cattle, etc.)
   - What is a ranch?
3. Read *Cowboys*.
4. Talk about what cowboys wear and let the children dress one on a flannel board.
5. Read *Ride 'Em, Cowboy*.
6. Play "Born to Ride." Lead the children on a pretend horse ride around the room.
7. Let's head west! Gather everyone and head to the western area.
8. First stop: the jail. Tell the children that this is where the bad cowboys go. If you are using their pictures, ask them if they recognize any of the cowboys on the "Wanted" posters.
9. Next stop: the ranch. Explain what goes on at the ranch and introduce children to the props.
10. Let's feed the horses. Take hay bales and apples over to the horses. Let the children pretend to feed them.
11. Time to round up the cattle! Let the children ride on the horses and try to round-up the "cows." You can tape an area on the floor and tell them to try to get all of the cows into the taped circle.
12. Trail ride! Let everyone take turns riding the horses along the path. Point out the western "landscape" and "animals" you see along the way.
13. Let's pan for gold! Let the children search for gold in the "panning" area.

14. It's nighttime! Show the children how to build the "campfire." Once the fire is built, gather everyone and pretend to eat like the cowboys do out on the trail...from a can.

15. Free play! Use the remainder of the time for free play, allowing the children to "work" around the ranch, ride the trails, search for gold, hang around the campfire, or sit in jail as they wish.

Final Thoughts

Providing a western pretend play day offers many ways for children to use their imaginations and foster the developmental skills they need to grow and learn about the world around them. While learning about life out west, children will also:

1. Use their imagination to discover ways to explore western life by using props such as pretend horses, a jail, a ranch and by conversing with others about western life during play.

2. Develop thinking skills as they consider how to "work" at a "ranch" and by using objects such as boxes and broomsticks for other purposes.

3. Enhance language skills as they listen to stories and songs that use specific vocabulary words pertaining to western life and by engaging in conversation with others.

4. Build social skills as they learn to share and play with others.

5. Exercise motor skills as they participate in interactive songs and physical play such as pretending to ride horses and round up cattle.

Let's Pretend: Pirates

Overview

Arrrrrr you ready for a pirate adventure? Grab your spyglass and treasure map and let's set sail. Pretending to be pirates offers lots of opportunity for role-play. "Let's Pretend: Pirates" offers ideas on how to take children on a pirate adventure using books, songs, props, and pirate-related activities.

Materials Needed

Props

Pirate Ship: box (large enough for several children to fit in), dowel, poster board
Paint the box brown. Attach a long dowel to one end. Make a pirate flag out of the poster board and attach to the dowel (see Figure 14.1).

Ocean: blue tarp, butcher paper, or blue cellophane
Use walls or furniture to hang blue tarp or butcher paper in a way that children can play under it (as if being under water).

Gold: cardboard
Cut round pieces from cardboard and paint gold.

Figure 14.1. Let's sail!

Treasure Chest: box, play jewelry, cardboard

Paint a box gold and fill it with play jewelry and "gold coins."

Sunken Ship: box

Paint a box brown and place it at the bottom of the "ocean." Hide a "treasure chest" in it.

Island: blanket or sheet

Use a brown or white blanket or sheet to mark off an "island" area beside the "ocean."

Eye Patch: construction paper, elastic

Cut a circle out of black construction paper and attach elastic (make it the correct size for a child's head).

Spyglass: paper towel roll

Plank: long piece of cardboard

Paint a piece of cardboard brown to look like a piece of wood. Place it beside the pirate ship, going into the "ocean."

Treasure Map: paper

Draw a map of the room (ocean, island, sunken ship, etc.). Place an "x" where the treasures are.

Miscellaneous: parrot, bandanas, fishing net

Books

Peck, Jan. *Pirate Treasure Hunt*. Gretna, LA: Pelican Publishing Co., Inc., 2008.

Sobel, June. *Shiver Me Letters*. Orlando: Harcourt, Inc., 2006.

Music

Allard, Peter T., and Ellen Allard. "Hello Everybody." *Sing It! Say It! Stamp It! Sway It! Volume 1* [CD]. Worcester, MA: 80-Z Music, 1999.

Captain Bogg and Salty. "The Plank Walker." *Emphatical Piratical* [CD]. Boston: Scabby-disc, 2009.

Pirates: Step-by-Step Example Program

1. Opening song: "Hello Everybody."
2. Talk with the children about pirates. Ask them questions such as:
   - What are pirates? (sail the seas, look for treasures, etc.)
   - What do they search for? (treasures, other ships, etc.)
   - What does walk the plank mean?
3. Read *Shiver Me Letters*.
4. Pirate Training. Tell the children that they have to learn how to be a pirate and do some practicing before they go on their adventure. Have them do things such as:
   - Practice saying "arrrr."
   - Make fierce faces.
   - Swim.

   Give them all a pirate patch upon completion of the "training."
5. Act out *Pirate Treasure Hunt*.
6. Walk the plank! Bring the children over to the plank and listen to "The Plank Walker" as they each get a turn walking the plank and jumping into the ocean.

7. We're all in the ocean! Tell them that you think there is a treasure map hidden in a sunken ship at the bottom of the sea. Tell everyone to swim down to the sunken ship to find the map.
8. Let's find that treasure! Swim to the island and, using the map, find the buried treasure.
9. Free play! Use the remainder of the time for free play, allowing the children to play as pirates and sail, swim, and look for treasures as they wish.

Final Thoughts

Pirate role-playing opens a lot of room for imaginative play and fosters the developmental skills children need to grow and learn about the world around them. While learning about pirates, children will also:

1. Use their imagination while playing with props such as boxes, blankets, and paper towel rolls to create a "pirate experience."
2. Develop thinking skills as they participate in activities such as treasure hunts and by using objects such as boxes and paper towel rolls for other purposes.
3. Enhance language skills by listening to stories about pirates and by engaging in conversation during play.
4. Build social skills by sharing and playing with others while pretending to be pirates.
5. Exercise motor skills as they participate in interactive songs and physical play such as "walking the plank" and swimming.

Let's Pretend: Apple Farm

Overview

It's apple-picking time! Grab your baskets and let's head out to the farm. "Let's Pretend: Apple Farm" offers ideas on how to set up a make-believe apple farm using books, songs, props, and apple farm-related activities.

Materials Needed

Props

Figure 15.1. Apple-picking time!

Figure 15.2. Let's buy apples!

Apple Trees: green and brown butcher paper or poster board, red and green construction paper

> Cut the brown paper into tree trunk shapes and the green paper into bushy treetop shapes. Place the green "foliage" at the top of the trunk. Make various sizes and tape them to the wall. Use red construction paper to make apples and tape them to the trees. Cut a slit in a few to add green worms made from construction paper (see Figure 15.1).

Apple Store: box, construction paper

> Use a box for an apple store. Cut out a window on one side and a door on another. Use construction paper to make a sign (see Figure 15.2).

Coins: cardboard

> Cut round pieces out of cardboard and spray paint silver or cover with foil.

Kitchen: 2 boxes

> Set up a kitchen area using a small box for a sink, stocked with an empty detergent bottle and a cloth to "wash" and "rinse" the apples. Cut an opening in the other box to make a door and use as an oven.

Apple Dessert: recipe, materials to make a pretend dessert, baked dessert

> Choose a recipe to bake ahead of time and also make a pretend one to "bake" in the "oven." An

example of a pretend dessert is an apple pizza, made from construction paper—beige or white circle for the pizza, red paper apple slices, and white shredded paper for icing.

Miscellaneous: bags/baskets, apples

Books

Esbensen, Barbara Juster. "Discovery." In *Swing Around the Sun*. Minneapolis, MN: Carolrhoda Books, Inc., 1965.

Hall, Zoe. *Apple Pie Tree*. New York: Scholastic, 1996.

Hubbell, Will. *Apples Here!* Morton Grove, IL: Albert, 2002.

Music

Allard, Peter T., and Ellen Allard. "Five Green Apples." *Sing It! Say It! Stamp It! Sway It! Volume 1* [CD]. Worcester, MA: 80-Z Music, 1999.

Allard, Peter T., and Ellen Allard. "Hello Everybody." *Sing It! Say It! Stamp It! Sway It! Volume 1* [CD]. Worcester, MA: 80-Z Music, 1999.

Apple Farm: A Step-by-Step Program Example

1. Opening song: "Hello Everybody."
2. Talk with the children about apples/apple farms. Ask them questions such as:
   - Where do apples come from? (grown on an apple tree; begin as a flower that turns into an apple)
   - What is an apple orchard? (place where apple trees grow, where people go to pick apples)
   - When do you pick apples? (fall)
3. Read *Apples Here!*
4. Listen to "Five Green Apples."
5. Read *Apple Pie Tree*.
6. Recite "Discovery," cutting an apple as you do so.
7. Let's go apple picking! Pretend to drive to the farm. Let's take a hayride out to the apple trees! (Pretend to bump up and down as you would on a wagon ride.)
8. Time to pick some apples! Give everyone a basket or a bag. Let everyone pick a few apples.
9. Let's pay! Let everyone line up at the store window to "pay" for their apples.
10. Baking time! Let everyone go over to the kitchen area to "wash" and "rinse" their apples.
11. Pretend to make a dessert (like the one you made ahead of time) and place it in the "oven."
12. Let's eat! Bring out the real dessert and enjoy.
13. Free play! Use the remainder of the time for free play, allowing the children to play in the "apple-farm" area as they wish.

Final Thoughts

Pretending to be at an apple farm offers a variety of ways to use the imagination for make-believe play and foster the developmental skills children need to grow and learn about the world around them. While learning about apple farms, children will also learn to:

1. Use their imaginations while playing with props such as a pretend orchard and apple store.
2. Develop thinking skills as they consider what goes on at an apple farm and as they use items such as boxes for various purposes.
3. Enhance language skills as they listen to stories, songs, and poems about apples and engage in pretend play.
4. Build social skills by learning to share and converse with other children while pretending to pick apples and bake.
5. Exercise motor skills as they participate in interactive songs and physical play such as "apple picking."

Let's Pretend:
Jungle Safari

Overview

Huge snakes, chattering monkeys, exotic birds…grab your cameras and binoculars. We're going on a jungle safari, without even going outside! "Let's Pretend: Jungle Safari" offers ideas on how to set up a jungle safari adventure using books, songs, props, and jungle/safari-related activities.

Materials Needed

Props

Jungle: 6 tables, green butcher paper
> Put approximately six tables end-to end, forming a U-shape. Tape the paper to all sides of the tables and shred it to look like grass.

Watering Hole: blue butcher paper or poster board
> Cut the paper to look pond/lake shaped. Place it outside the "jungle" (see Figure 16.1).

Tiki Hut: box, newspaper, rubber bands, brown paint
> Collect enough newspapers to roll and cover a box big enough for a child to get inside. Keep each paper rolled by putting a rubber band around the middle. Glue the newspaper rolls to the box and paint brown (see Figure 16.2).

Binoculars: toilet paper rolls, yarn
> Attach yarn to two toilet paper rolls by punching a hole in each roll and making a knot in the yarn to keep it from sliding through the hole (see Figure 16.3).

Animal Masks

Safari Hats

Miscellaneous: vines, stuffed animals (snakes, monkeys, etc.), insects
> Hang these items throughout the "jungle."

Figure 16.1. Wild animals love a watering hole!

Figure 16.2. A tiki hut in the jungle

Figure 16.3. Looking for animals on a wild safari!

Books

Ashman, Linda. *Starry Safari*. New York: Harcourt, Inc., 2005.

Beaton, Clare. *How Loud Is a Lion?* Cambridge, MA: Barefoot Books, 2002.

Music

Allard, Peter T., and Ellen Allard. "Hello Everybody." *Sing It! Say It! Stamp It! Sway It! Volume 1* [CD]. Worcester, MA: 80-Z Music, 1999.

Banana Slug String Band. "Animals Are Dancing." *Penguin Parade* [CD]. Redway, CA: Music for the Little People, 1995.

Jungle Safari: A Step-by-Step Program Example

1. Opening song: "Hello Everybody."
2. Talk with the children about the jungle. Ask them questions such as:
   - What is a jungle?
   - What animals live in a jungle?
   - What do you do on a safari?
3. Read *Starry Safari*.
4. Listen/dance to "Animals Are Dancing."
5. Read *How Loud Is a Lion?*
6. Safari time! Begin at the tiki hut and pass out hats, binoculars, and masks (to those children who want to pretend to be jungle animals rather than explorers). Lead them through the "jungle," showing them different "animals" and "insects" along the way. Stop at the "watering hole" for a break.
7. Free play! Use the remainder of the time for free play, allowing the children to explore the jungle, play in the tiki hut, or pretend to be animals.

Final Thoughts

Setting up a jungle safari allows great opportunity for children to use their imaginations and foster the developmental skills children need to grow and learn about the world around them. While learning about jungle life and safari fun, children will also:

1. Use their imaginations to explore jungle life during play.
2. Develop thinking skills as they participate in activities such as looking for various "animals" in the "jungle."
3. Enhance language skills as they listen to stories and songs pertaining to jungles/safaris and converse with each other during play.
4. Build social skills as they share props and engage in conversation.
5. Exercise motor skills as they participate in interactive songs and physical play such as crawling through the "jungle."

PROGRAM **17**

Let's Pretend: Under the Sea

Overview

The ocean is like another world in comparison to life on land. What better way to introduce children to ocean life than by creating an underwater world for them to explore. "Let's Pretend: Under the Sea" offers ideas on how to set up an ocean using books, songs, props, and ocean-related activities.

Materials Needed

Props

Ocean: blue tarp, butcher paper, or blue cellophane
  Use walls or furniture to hang blue tarp, butcher paper, or blue cellophane in a way that children can play under it (as if being under water).

Sea Shells: printed pictures or real shells
  Print seashell pictures on the computer or use real shells. Place them at the "bottom of the ocean."

Jellyfish: balloons, streamers
  Blow up balloons and attach streamers to them.

Clams: 2 pie pans, brads, cotton balls, construction paper or glue-on eyes
  Attach two pie pans together on one side with a brad and cover the bottom with cotton balls. Glue a piece of white fabric over the cotton balls. Make a face with glue-on eyes or construction paper (see Figure 17.1).

Figure 17.1. A happy clam

Starfish: sandpaper
  Cut star chapes out of sandpaper.

Baby Octopus: toilet paper roll
  Make eight cuts around the roll for legs. Bend/curl the legs to spread them out. Draw a face (see Figure 17.2).

Fish: paper plates
  Cut a triangular shape out of one side of the plate to make a mouth. Attach the triangle to the other side of the plate to make a fin. Decorate.

Figure 17.2. A baby octopus

Treasure Chest: box, treasures, and Styrofoam peanuts
Paint a box to look like a treasure chest. Fill it with stuffed peanuts and treasures and place at the bottom of the "ocean."
Submarine: box
Use a box big enough for one or more children to get in. Paint and decorate it to look like a submarine.

Books

Rose, Deborah Lee. *Ocean Babies*. Washington, DC: National Geographic, 2005.
Sherry, Kevin. *I'm the Biggest Thing in the Ocean*. New York: Dial Books for Young Readers, 2007.

Music

Allard, Peter T., and Ellen Allard. "Hello Everybody." *Sing It! Say It! Stamp It! Sway It! Volume 1* [CD]. Worcester, MA: 80-Z Music, 1999.
Downing, Johnette. "Clamshell Clap." *Fins and Grins* [CD]. New Orleans: Wiggle Worm Records, 2006.
Sangiolo, Maria. "Down by the Ocean." *Under the Mystic Sea* [CD]. Pomfret, CT: Raging River Records, 2007.

Under the Sea: A Step-by-Step Program Example

1. Opening song: "Hello Everybody."
2. Talk with the children about ocean life. Ask them questions such as:
   • What are oceans/difference between them and a pond/lake?
   • What lives in the ocean? (fish, shark, etc.)
3. Read *Ocean Babies*.
4. Listen to "Clamshell Clap."
5. Read *I'm the Biggest Thing in the Ocean*.
6. Listen/act out verses to "Down by the Ocean."
7. Grab your goggles (make with hands over your eyes) and let's explore the ocean! Lead the children to the ocean.
8. Let's explore! Lead the children on a swim to the bottom of the "sea," stopping to introduce them to the various sea life.
9. A treasure chest! Dig to see what you can find.
10. A submarine! Show them the submarine and how/why it is used.
11. Free play! Use the remainder of the time for free play, allowing the children to explore the "ocean" and play in the submarine.

Final Thoughts

A make-believe ocean offers a lot of room for children to use their imaginations and foster the developmental skills they need to grow and learn about the world around them. While they learn about ocean life, children will also:

1. Use their imaginations to explore "under the sea" by using props and engaging in conversation.

2. Develop thinking skills as they learn about ocean life and use items such as pie pans, balloons, and toilet paper rolls for other purposes.
3. Enhance language skills by listening to stories and songs that use vocabulary words pertaining to oceans and by conversing with others during play.
4. Build social skills by sharing props and talking with other children during play.
5. Exercise motor skills as they participate in interactive songs and physical play such as pretend swimming.

Let's Pretend: In a Fantasy Land

Overview

Fantasy is the essence of imagination. Give children the opportunity to explore a magical world by creating a fantasy land. "Let's Pretend: In a Fantasy Land" offers ideas on how to set up a world of fantasy complete with a castle, magic wands, and crowns by using books, songs, props, and fantasy-related activities.

Materials Needed

Props

Figure 18.1. A magical castle

Figure 18.2. A magical fairy garden

Castle: box(es), rope

Cut rectangular crenellations along the top of the box(es). Cut out a drawbridge door on one side, leaving it attached to the box. Add a rope to each side of the door and adjoining wall. Cut window(s) on the other sides of the box(es). If you are attaching several boxes together to make a larger castle, cut out the interior walls of all three boxes, leaving enough cardboard to attach the boxes with brads (see Figure 18.1).

Fairy Garden: poster board, cardboard, pictures of fairies, butterflies, flowers, and netting

Use a piece of cardboard to make a picket fence. Cut various sizes of mushrooms out of different colored poster board, using white poster board for the stems. Hang netting to make a fairy bower. Tape pictures of fairies, butterflies, and flowers throughout the area (see Figure 18.2).

Magic Wands: straws, construction paper, ribbon, glitter

Cut stars out of construction paper and decorate with glitter. Glue the stars to straws. Tie ribbons around the straws.

Crowns: construction paper, glitter

Cut a crown out of construction paper and decorate. Attach the two ends together.

Knight Costume: pillowcase, coat of arms picture
Cut three holes in the pillowcase along the seam and sides for the head and arms. Cut rectangular shapes around the bottom. Glue a coat of arms picture to the front (see Figure 18.3).
Wizard Hat: construction paper, glitter, string
Fold paper into a cone shape. Use paper and glitter to decorate the hat (stars and moons look nice). Attach a string to hold the hat in place on the child's head.
Wizard Box: box with lid, plastic containers, snakes, rocks
Attach the lid to the box so that it opens like a chest. Decorate and fill with things for "potions and spells" such as snakes and rocks. The plastic containers are to be used to make potions (see Figure 18.4).

Books

Mayhew, James. *Who Wants a Dragon?* New York: Orchard Books, Scholastic Inc., 2004
Prelutsky, Jack. *The Wizard.* New York: Greenwillow Books, 1976.

Music

Allard, Peter T., and Ellen Allard. "Hello Everybody." *Sing It! Say It! Stamp It! Sway It! Volume 1* [CD]. Worcester, MA: 80-Z Music, 1999.
Ronno. "5 Brave Knights." *Castles, Knights, and Unicorns* [CD]. Long Branch, NJ: Kimbo Educational, 2001.
Sangiolo, Maria. "Fairy Ring." *Fairy Moon* [CD]. Pomfret, CT: Raging River Records, 2004.

Figure 18.3. I'm ready to defeat a dragon!

Figure 18.4. A wizard's necessities

In a Fantasy Land: A Step-by-Step Program Example

1. Opening song: "Hello Everybody."
2. Talk with the children about fantasy lands. Ask them questions such as:
   - What would you find in a fantasy land? (castles, dragons, fairies, wizards, etc.)
   - What do wizards do? (create magical spells)
   - Where do fairies live? (flowers, mushrooms, etc.)
3. Read *Who Wants a Dragon?*
4. Use "5 Brave Knights" as a fingerplay.
5. Read *The Wizard.*
6. Form a circle and dance to "Fairy Ring."
7. Let's explore a magical land! Begin at the castle, where the children can either make their own crowns/wizard hats/magic wands, or you can let them choose premade ones.

8. We need a magic potion! Show them the potion/spell supplies in the wizard box and let them help create some magic. Be sure to use your wand!
9. Let's look for fairies! Bring the children over to the fairy garden. Shh! You have to be very quiet. Let the children look for the fairies hidden among the flowers and mushrooms.
10. Free play! Use the remainder of the time for free play, allowing the children to use the various props to explore this fantasy land.

Final Thoughts

Creating a fantasy land allows a variety of ways for children to use their imaginations and foster the developmental skills they need to grow and learn about the world around them. While learning about different elements of fantasy, children will also:

1. Use their imaginations to explore a "magical world" by using props such as wands and wizard hats and by role-playing with others.
2. Develop thinking skills as they use props and conversation to participate in play.
3. Enhance language skills as they listen to stories and songs about fantasy elements and engage in conversation during play.
4. Build social skills as they share props such as the wizard box and castle while contributing to pretend play.
5. Exercise motor skills by participating in interactive songs and physical play.

Let's Pretend:
On a Boat Trip

Overview

Row, row, row your boat...across the lake and down the river. Grab your oars and let's go on a boating adventure. "Let's Pretend: On a Boat Trip" offers ideas on how to set up a boat trip and take children on an outing using books, songs, props, and boat-related activities without ever touching water.

Materials Needed

Props

Lake: blue tarp
> Spread a large blue tarp across the floor.

Island: brown, beige, or white blanket
> Spread a brown, beige, or white sheet/blanket in the middle of the "lake."

River: blue butcher paper, or several pieces of blue poster board
> Place a long strip of blue butcher paper or several pieces of blue poster board on the floor, leading away from the "lake."

Rocks: crumbled newspaper, white/gray sheet
> Make several piles of crumbled newspaper throughout the "river." Place a white or gray sheet over the newspaper piles.

Boat: box (large enough for several children to fit in), 2 large pieces of cardboard, paint

> Use the two large pieces of cardboard to make the bow of the boat by attaching them together (hot glue works well) and then attaching them to one end of the box. Paint the box as you wish and then paint "water" along the bottom of the box (see Figure 19.1).

Figure 19.1. Row, row, row your boat!

Oars: cardboard
> Cut oar shapes out of cardboard.

Anchor: cardboard
> Cut an anchor out of cardboard and attach a rope to it.

Picnic Supplies: basket, blanket, empty food containers/fake food.

Scenery: construction paper or printed pictures
> Place tree cutouts and pictures of wildlife along the wall.

Books

McDonnell, Flora. *I Love Boats*. Cambridge, MA: Candlewick Press, 1995.

Trapani, Iza. *Row, Row, Row Your Boat*. Dallas, TX: Whispering Coyote Press, 1999.

Music

Allard, Peter T., and Ellen Allard. "Hello Everybody." *Sing It! Say It! Stamp It! Sway It! Volume 1* [CD]. Worcester, MA: 80-Z Music, 1999.

Molloy, Sukey. "Row, Row, Row Your Boat." *Circle Songs* [CD]. 2005.

On a Boat Trip: A Step-by-Step Program Example

1. Opening song: "Hello Everybody."
2. Talk with the children about boats. Ask them questions such as:
   - Where would you ride in a boat? (lake, river, ocean, etc.)
   - What are boats for? (boat trips, transporting things, etc.)
3. Read *Row, Row, Row Your Boat*.
4. Grab a partner. Sit facing each other and hold hands. Listen to "Row, Row, Row Your Boat" as you "row" together.
5. Read *I Love Boats*.
6. Water safety first! Teach the children to "swim" (doggie paddle, stroke, etc.) just in case the boat flips! Tell them they should always wear a life jacket and pretend to put one on.
7. Grab your oars! Show them how to use the oars and then pass them out to each child. If you don't have enough to use for everyone at the same time, just pretend.
8. Let's go! Because everyone won't be able to fit in the boat at once, use a pretend boat during this time. Line everyone up and pretend to be in a boat. Use the "oars" to paddle across the "lake" and don't forget to bring the picnic basket.
9. Break time! Take a break on the island and enjoy a picnic lunch.
10. Braving the river. Return to the pretend boat and lead everyone back across the lake to the river. Take the children down the river, avoiding the "big rocks." Don't forget to admire the scenery!
11. Free play! Use the remainder of the time for free play, allowing the children to take a leisurely ride on the lake or an adventurous journey down the river.

Final Thoughts

Setting up a make-believe boat trip is a great way to encourage children to use their imaginations and foster developmental skills they need to grow and learn about the world around them. While learning about boats, children will also:

1. Use their imaginations while playing with props such as boxes and pretend scenery to create a boating adventure.
2. Develop thinking skills as they use items such as boxes for other purposes and engage in conversation.
3. Enhance language skills as they listen to stories and songs about boats and converse with others during play.
4. Build social skills as they share props and take part in pretend play.
5. Exercise motor skills as they participate in interactive songs and physical play such as "rowing a boat."

Let's Pretend: Outer Space

Overview

It's not every day you get an opportunity to go out in space. However, with a little imagination, you can strap a jetpack to your back and soar around the universe! "Let's Pretend: Outer Space" offers ideas on how to introduce children to life in the cosmos with a story, song, props, and space-related activities.

Materials Needed

Props

Moon Area: newspaper, pillows, bubble wrap, gray/white sheet

Cover piles of crumpled newspaper, pillows, bubble wrap etc., with a gray/white sheet.

Space Station: box, plastic bottle caps, foil, cords, old phone

Remove one side and the bottom of the box so that you have a stand. Paint the box black and cover some of the bottle caps with foil. Glue the bottle caps onto the cardboard for knobs. Attach an old phone cord to the cardboard and place an old phone at the "stand."

Figure 20.1. Lil' astronauts

Space Helmets: grocery bag, markers

Turn the bag upside down and cut out a circle (about the size of a child's face) on the front. Decorate it with markers (see Figure 20.1).

Jetpacks: cereal box, 2 paper towel rolls, red/yellow/orange tissue paper, yarn, silver/gray paint

Glue a paper towel roll on each side of the cereal box and paint silver/gray. Attach a piece of yarn on each side to make straps that will fit over a child's shoulders. Stuff red/yellow/orange tissue paper into the bottom of the paper towel roll for "flames" (see Figure 20.2).

Flying Saucer: pie pan, construction paper

Turn a pie pan upside down. Cut out different shapes on the construction paper and glue around the "saucer."

Figure 20.2. Ready to soar!

Alien Puppet: 2 plastic bowls with lips, glove, googly eyes, pipe cleaner

Punch a hole on each bowl's lip and line them up so that one bowl will be upside down. Run a pipe cleaner through the holes to attach the bowls together. Cut a hole in the bottom of one of the bowls big enough for a hand to fit through. Glue two googly eyes and two small pieces of pipe cleaner on each finger of the glove. The glove will go up through the hole in the bottom of the bowl during play (see Figure 20.3).

Figure 20.3. Aliens

Miscellaneous: fishing line to hang planets, stars, and comets around the area; foil to cover tables

Books

Loomis, Christine. *Astro Bunnies*. New York: G.P Putnam's Sons, 2001.

Music

Allard, Peter T., and Ellen Allard. "Hello Everybody." *Sing It! Say It! Stamp It! Sway It! Volume 1* [CD]. Worcester, MA: 80-Z Music, 1999.

Laurie Berkner Band. "Rocketship Run." *Rocketship Run* [CD]. New York: Two Tomatoes, 2008.

Other

"5 Little Aliens" (*Tune*: "10 Little Indians")

1 little, 2 little, 3 little aliens.
4 little, 5 little funny aliens.
Land on Earth to look around
And then decide to leave the ground.

Outer Space: A Step-by-Step Program Example

1. Opening song: "Hello Everybody."
2. Talk with the children about space. Ask them questions such as:
   - What is in outer space? (moons, stars, comets, planets, etc.)
   - Who travels there? (astronauts)
   - How do astronauts get there? (rocket)
3. Read *Astro Bunnies*.
4. Recite "5 Little Aliens" using the alien puppet.
5. Listen to "Rocketship Run" and soar around the storytime area.
6. Time for an outer space adventure! Give each child a jetpack.
7. First stop: the moon. Let each child explore the moon as he or she tries to walk over the bubble wrap, pillows, and crumpled newspaper.
8. Next stop: space station/control panel. Show the children how to "operate" the panel. Be sure to "refuel" your packs.
9. Return to Earth.
10. Free play! Use the remainder of the time for free play, allowing the children to explore "outer space" as they choose.

Additional Props

Spaceship

Use a box to make a space ship.

Starscope

Use a paper towel tube to make a starscope.

Moonbuggy

Use an egg carton to make a moonbuggy.

Final Thoughts

Creating a make-believe outer space offers tremendous opportunity for children to use their imaginations and foster the developmental skills they need to grow and learn about the world around them. While learning about life in the cosmos, children will also:

1. Use their imaginations as they use items such as boxes, grocery bags, and bottle caps for other purposes to create an outer space experience.
2. Develop thinking skills as they consider life in outer space and use props to "explore the moon" and "operate a control panel."
3. Enhance language skills as they listen to music and a story about outer space and engage in conversation during pretend play.
4. Build social skills as they share props and converse with others.
5. Exercise motor skills as they participate in interactive song and physical play such as flying in their "jetpacks" and walking on the "moon."

Let's Pretend:
A Fall Day

Overview

There is so much to do during the autumn season. Rake leaves. Play in leaf piles. Pick apples. Go on hayrides on a crisp night. "Let's Pretend: A Fall Day" offers ideas on how to create a fall day indoors using books, songs, props, and fall-related activities.

Figure 21.1. Let's build a scarecrow!

Materials Needed

Props

Leaves: real leaves or construction paper

Make big piles with real leaves or cut out leaves from red, yellow, brown, and orange construction paper and scatter around.

Apple Trees: green and brown butcher paper or poster board, red and green construction paper

Cut the brown paper into tree trunk shapes and the green paper into bushy treetop shapes. Place the green "foliage" at the top of the trunk. Make various sizes and tape them to the wall. Use red construction paper to make apples and tape them to the trees. Cut a slit in a few to add green worms made from construction paper (see Figure 15.1, p. 42).

Pumpkin Patch: rectangular boxes, crumpled/ shredded newspaper painted brown, fake vine, orange balloons

Fill several small rectangular boxes with newspaper (dirt). Blow up the balloons and tape the tie part to the vine. Place them in the pumpkin patch (see Figure 26.1, p. 70).

Scarecrow: newspaper, pants, shirt, boots, hat, pillowcase

Stuff the pants, shirt, and pillowcase with newspaper. Tie the pillowcase and tuck it into the neck of the shirt. Tuck the shirt into the pants. Place the boots over the pants leg. Draw a face on the pillowcase and add a hat (see Figure 21.1).

Books

Hall, Zoe. *Fall Leaves Fall!* New York: Scholastic Press, 2000.
Nidey, Kelli. *When Autumn Falls.* Morton Grove, IL: Albert Whitman and Company, 2004.

Music

Allard, Peter T., and Ellen Allard. "Hello Everybody." *Sing It! Say It! Stamp It! Sway It! Volume 1* [CD]. Worcester, MA: 80-Z Music, 1999.

Frezza, Rebecca, and Big Truck. "Leaves Are Falling." *Special Kind of Day* [CD]. Big Truck Music, 2008.

A Fall Day: A Step-by-Step Program Example

1. Opening song: "Hello Everybody."
2. Talk with the children about the autumn season. Ask them questions such as:
   - What happens in the fall? (leaves turn colors and fall, air gets cooler, etc.)
   - What can you do in the fall? (pick apples, play in leaves, etc.)
3. Read *Fall Leaves Fall!*
4. Sprinkle "leaves" on the children as you listen to "Leaves Are Falling."
5. Read *When Autumn Falls.*
6. Let's enjoy our "Fall Day." Play in the leaves. Make piles to jump in.
7. We must have a scarecrow! Work together to build the scarecrow.
8. Time to pick some delicious apples. Lead the children over to the apple trees and let them pick some apples. Be sure to look for worms!
9. What about a pumpkin? Bring them to the "pumpkin patch" and pick some pumpkins. Give them black markers to draw faces on the pumpkins.
10. Free play! Use the remainder of the time for free play, allowing the children to enjoy their "Fall Day" as they choose.

Final Thoughts

Because there is so much to do during the autumn season, creating a pretend "Fall Day" offers a lot of room for children to use their imaginations and foster the developmental skills they need to grow and learn about the world around them. While learning about fall time, children will also:

1. Use their imaginations as they play with props such as pretend pumpkins and scarecrows to create an autumn experience.
2. Develop thinking skills as they participate in activities such as building a scarecrow and using items such as balloons for imaginative play.
3. Enhance language skills as they listen to stories and songs that use vocabulary words pertaining to the autmn season and by conversing with others during play.
4. Build social skills as they use the props to play together, such as in building a scarecrow.
5. Exercise motor skills as they participate in interactive songs and physical play such as "playing in leaves" and "picking apples."

Let's Pretend: In the Garden

Overview

Vegetables, flowers, so much to pick! Rock gardens, children's gardens, gardens for sticks? There are so many types of gardens to discover. "Let's Pretend: In the Garden" offers ideas on how to set up different types of gardens for children to explore using books, songs, props, and garden-related activities.

Materials Needed

Props

Flower Garden: rectangular boxes, crumpled/shredded newspaper painted brown, construction paper, cardboard

Fill several small rectangular boxes with the newspaper paper (dirt). Make construction paper flowers (or print pictures from the computer) and glue them to cardboard for support. Stick the flowers in the "dirt." Spray fragrance on a few. Add paper butterflies and other insects to the area (see Figure 22.1).

Figure 22.1. Let's pick flowers

Vegetable Garden: rectangular boxes, crumpled/shredded paper, construction paper, cardboard, fake plants, long sock/legging

Fill several rectangular boxes with the newspaper paper (dirt). Make vegetables out of construction paper (or print pictures from the computer) and glue them to cardboard for support. Stick the root vegetable into the "dirt" and hang the others on fake plants. Add paper insects and stuff a long sock or legging to make a snake to hide in the garden.

Rock Garden: boxes, Styrofoam peanuts, blue poster board, construction paper

Use several short boxes to make one big box and fill with Styrofoam peanuts. Decorate boxes to make "sculptures" and place throughout the garden. Use blue poster board to make a "pool" and add lily pads made from construction paper. Complete the garden with flowers made from construction paper or pictures printed from the computer.

Watering Can: empty cylinder container (oatmeal container works well), toilet paper roll

Cut one end of the toilet paper roll at an angle and glue to the container. Paint/decorate as desired.

Rake, Shovel, Hoe: wrapping paper roll, cardboard

Cut a piece of cardboard to look like a rake, shovel, and hoe. Attach a wrapping paper tube for the handle.

Books

Brenner, Barbara. *Good Morning, Garden*. Chanhassen, MN: NorthWord Press, 2004.

Dahl, Michael. *From the Garden*. Minneapolis: Picture Window Books, 2004.

Music

Allard, Peter T., and Ellen Allard. "Hello Everybody." *Sing It! Say It! Stamp It! Sway It! Volume 1* [CD]. Worcester, MA: 80-Z Music, 1999.

Raffi. "In My Garden." *One Light, One Sun* [CD]. Universal City, CA: MCA Records, 1985.

In the Garden: A Step-by-Step Program Example

1. Opening song: "Hello Everybody."
2. Talk with the children about gardens. Ask them questions such as:
   - What types of gardens are there? (flower, vegetable, sculpture, etc.)
   - What are some tools used to maintain a garden? (rake, hoe, shovel, etc.)
3. Read *Good Morning, Garden*.
4. Play "In My Garden" and act out the verses.
5. Read *From the Garden*.
6. Let's go on a garden tour! First garden: flower garden. Take the children on a walk through the garden and point out the different flowers and insects. Let them try to find the fragrant flowers.
7. Next garden: vegetable garden. Talk about what kinds of vegetable are in the garden and pick the ripe ones. Don't forget to water everything! And watch out for the snake!
8. Last stop: the rock garden. Talk about how this garden is different from the other two. Discuss the sculptures and what you see in the pool.
9. Free play! Use the remainder of the time for free play, allowing the children to play and work in the gardens as they choose.

Final Thoughts

Creating make-believe gardens offers children a lot of opportunity to use their imaginations and foster the developmental skills they need to grow and learn about the world around them. While learning about gardens, they will also:

1. Use their imaginations to explore different types of gardens using props.
2. Develop thinking skills as they consider the different types of gardens and use items such as Styrofoam peanuts and boxes for various purposes.

3. Enhance language skills as they listen to stories and songs about gardens and engage in conversation.
4. Build social skills as they share props such as gardening tools and converse with others during play.
5. Exercise motor skills as they participate in interactive songs and physical play such as pretend gardening.

Let's Pretend: Birthday Party

Overview

It's a birthday party and everyone's invited! Who is the guest of honor? Mr. Fuzzy. "Let's Pretend: Birthday Party" offers ideas on how to set up a make-believe birthday party for Mr. Fuzzy, the teddy bear, using a book, songs, props, and birthday party-related activities.

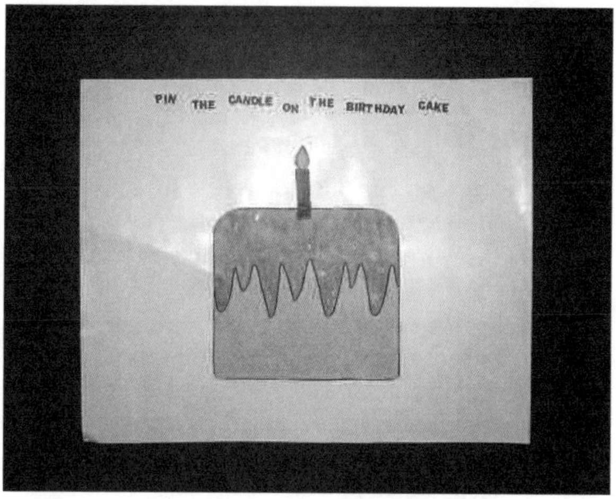

Materials Needed

Props

Parade: musical instruments, streamers, confetti, bubbles
  See Program 5 for ideas.
Presents: balloons, boxes, newspaper (comic section)
  Place a blown-up balloon in each box and wrap with the newspaper.
Pin-the-Candle-on-the-Cake: poster board, construction paper, blindfold
  Draw a birthday cake on a piece of poster board. Make a candle out of construction paper and laminate if possible (see Figure 23.1).

Figure 23.1. Pin the candle on the birthday cake!

Cake Recipe
Teddy Bear (guest of honor)
Miscellaneous: balloons, confetti, streamers, bubbles

Books

Boynton, Sandra. *Birthday Monsters.* New York: Workman Publishing, 1993.

Music

Allard, Peter T., and Ellen Allard. "Hello Everybody." *Sing It! Say It! Stamp It! Sway It! Volume 1* [CD]. Worcester, MA: 80-Z Music, 1999.
Hilderbrand, Karen Mitzo, and Kim Mitzo Thompson. "It's Your Special Day Parade." *Birthday Party Songs* [CD]. Twin Sisters Productions IP, LLC, 2001.
Nee, Judy. "The Balloon Game." *Birthday Party Singalong* [CD]. Redway, CA: Music for Little People, 2001.

Birthday Party: A Step-by-Step Program Example

1. Opening song: "Hello Everybody."
2. Talk about birthday parties with the children and tell them that you will be having a pretend birthday party for Mr. Fuzzy. Ask them questions such as:
   - What do you do at birthday parties? (eat cake, open presents, play games, etc.)
3. Read *Birthday Monsters*.
4. Birthday parade! Play "It's Your Special Day Parade" and use musical instruments, streamers, bubbles, etc., as you march around the room.
5. Gift time! Place Mr. Fuzzy at the head of the circle and let everyone open a balloon gift.
6. Balloon game! Use the balloon gifts and play "The Balloon Game."
7. Pin the candle on the cake! Make a line and give each blindfolded child a chance to play pin-the-candle-on-the-cake.
8. Cake time! Bring out the birthday cake and enjoy!
9. Free play! Use the remainder of the time for free play, allowing the children to play and socialize as they wish.

Final Thoughts

Throwing a pretend birthday party for a teddy bear gives children the opportunity to use their imaginations and foster the developmental skills they need to grow and learn about the world around them. Children will:

1. Use their imaginations as they use pretend gifts to celebrate.
2. Develop thinking skills as they consider what happens at a birthday party.
3. Enhance language skills as they listen to stories/songs and converse with others during play.
4. Build social skills as they share props with others and engage in conversation.
5. Exercise motor skills as they participate in interactive songs and physical play such as marching in the parade.

Let's Pretend: A Haunted House

Overview

Boo! But don't be scared. "Let's Pretend: A Haunted House" offers ideas on how to create a haunted house with fun, not frightening, books, songs, props and haunted house–related activities for a spooktacular time.

Materials Needed

Props

Haunted House: box, several tables, black butcher paper
   Cut two entrances in a large box (appliance size) and place it flush with a table. Line several tables up to form an "L" shape. Tape black butcher paper along the sides to make walls.

Spooky Trees: bare branches, black paint, pots, orange lights
   Paint the branches black and place in the pots. Wrap orange lights around them. Place the trees at the entrance to the haunted house.

Spider Web: stuffing/spider webbing
   Stretch the stuffing/webbing out and attach it to walls, corners, and furniture with tape. Place several throughout the haunted house.

Spider: 4-hole black button, 4 pipe cleaners
   Use four pipe cleaners to lace through two holes and bend them for legs. Stick some spiders in webs and place others randomly throughout the haunted house (see Figure 24.1).

Figure 24.1. Eeek! A spider!

Witch Mobile: wire hanger, black and orange construction paper, fishing line
   Make a circular shape out of the hanger. Cut out black witches on brooms and an orange crescent moon. Use fishing line to hang the witches on the hanger and to hang the hanger in the haunted house's box entrance.

Jack-o-Lanterns: orange balloons
   Draw faces on the blown up balloons with black marker. Place some at the entrance to the haunted house and others throughout the inside of the house.

Ghosts: tissue, fishing line
   Make a ball with a tissue and place in the middle of another tissue. Use fishing line to tie the tissue around the ball. Use a marker to draw a funny face on the ghost. Hang it with fishing line. Hang the ghosts throughout the haunted house.

Feely Box: tissue box, cellophane
   Line the tissue box with cellophane. Fill it with items such as grapes, spaghetti, and canned peaches. Place the box(es) throughout the haunted house.

Miscellaneous: cauldron (and things to put in it like snakes and insects), brooms, orange lights, roll of toilet paper, masks

Books

Bunting, Eve. *In the Haunted House*. New York: Clarion Books, 1990.
Mitton, Tony. *Spooky Hour*. New York: Orchard Books, 2003.

Music

Allard, Peter T., and Ellen Allard. "Hello Everybody." *Sing It! Say It! Stamp It! Sway It! Volume 1* [CD]. Worcester, MA: 80-Z Music, 1999.
Frezza, Rebecca, and Big Truck. "Spooky Dance." *A Special Kind of Day* [CD]. Big Truck Music, 2008.
"If You're Scary and You Know It." *Spooky Favorites* [CD]. Redway, CA: Music for Little People, 1999.

A Haunted House: A Step-by-Step Program Example

1. Opening song: "Hello Everybody."
2. Talk about haunted houses with the children. Ask them questions such as:
   • What do you find in a haunted house? (ghosts, spiders, etc.)
3. Read *In the Haunted House*.
4. Listen/dance to "If You're Scary and You Know It."
5. Read *Spooky Hour*.
6. Listen/dance to "Spooky Dance."
7. Who wants to be a mummy? Use toilet paper to wrap a volunteer like a mummy.
8. Let's brave the haunted house. Lead the children through the house. Watch out for those spider webs. Ooooh, see the ghosts? Let them try to guess what is in the feely boxes.
9. A witch has cast a spell on us; we're spiders! Go back through the haunted house, crawling like a spider (on hands and feet with your rear up in the air).
10. Free play! Use the remainder of the time as free play, allowing the children to brew stuff in the cauldron, make more mummies, and use masks to play as ghouls in the haunted house.

Final Thoughts

Creating a "haunted house" for children to play in allows them to use their imaginations and foster the developmental skills they need to grow and learn about the world around them. Children will:

1. Use their imaginations as they use props to create spooky play.
2. Develop thinking skills as they participate in activities such as guessing what is in the feely boxes and use items such as balloons, tissue, and tables for other purposes.
3. Enhance language skills as they listen to spooky stories and songs and converse with others.
4. Build social skills as they share props and engage in conversation during play.
5. Exercise motor skills as they participate in interactive songs and physical play such as crawling through the haunted house as a spider.

Let's Pretend: At the Airport

Overview

Airports and airplanes generate excitement in children of all ages. Creating a make-believe airport and taking children on a pretend airplane ride is a great way to encourage children to use their imaginations. "Let's Pretend: At the Airport" offers ideas on how to set up a make-believe airport using books, songs, props, and airport/airplane-related activities.

Materials Needed

Props

Airplane: large rectangular box, cardboard

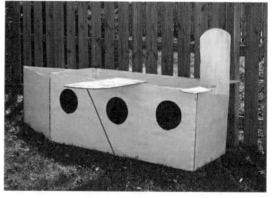

Figure 25.1. Let's fly!

> Place the box lengthwise. Use the cardboard to make wings and attach to each side of the box. Cut holes or paint black circles on the sides for windows and create an entrance (see Figure 25.1).

Terminal: table, bedsheet

> Place the end of the table flush with one side of the "plane." Cover it with a sheet.

Arrival/Departure Monitor: box, sheet of paper

> Paint the box black. Make a list of arrival and departure times on the paper and glue the paper to the box.

Boarding Passes: scrap paper

> Write "Pass" on strips of scrap paper.

Luggage Tickets: scrap paper and tape

> Tape strips of scrap paper to luggage.

Luggage: boxes

Security: 2 tables

> Place two tables end-to-end with just enough space to walk between them.

Baggage Claim: table

Patrol Signals: 2 paper towel rolls

> Paint the paper towel rolls to look more realistic, if desired.

Scenery: poster board and tape

> Cut out a sun and clouds from poster board and tape to the wall beside the airplane.

Books

Hubbell, Patricia. *Airplanes*. Tarrytown, NY: Marshall Cavendish Corporation, 2008.
Ormerod, Jan. *Miss Mouse Takes Off*. New York: HarperCollins Publishers, 2001.

Music

Allard, Peter T., and Ellen Allard. "Hello Everybody." *Sing It! Say It! Stamp It! Sway It! Volume 1* [CD]. Worcester, MA: 80-Z Music, 1999.

Other

"Going on a Big Airplane" (*Tune*: "The Wheels on the Bus")

The wheels on our car go 'round and 'round, 'round and 'round, 'round and 'round
(*Repeat.*)
Going to the airport.
We walk and we walk down the ramp, down the ramp, down the ramp
(*Repeat.*)
Going on a big airplane.
(*Walk your hands on your knees.*)
The ticket taker reads our pass, reads our pass, reads our pass
(*Repeat.*)
Going on a big airplane.
(*Pretend to read, hands together, palms up.*)
We find our seat with the little window, little window, little window
(*Repeat.*)
Going on a big airplane.
(*Make a window with your thumb and pointer finger.*)
The flight attendant says "Buckle your belt, buckle your belt, buckle your belt"
(*Repeat.*)
Going on a big airplane.
(*Put hands across tummy and bump fingers together.*)

Say to the children:

"I think we're starting to move. I think the wheels are starting to go around
very fast
(*Make a slow wheel moving motion with your hands.*)
The wheels on the plane go 'round and 'round, 'round and 'round, 'round and 'round
(*Sing and repeat slowly.*)

At the Airport: A Step-by-Step Program Example

1. Opening song: "Hello Everybody."
2. Talk with the children about airplanes and airports. Ask them questions such as:
   - What are airports? (where planes land and take off)
   - Who "drives" a plane? (pilot)
   - Where does a plane go? (flies in the sky)
3. Read *Airplanes*.
4. Sing/act out "Going on a Big Airplane."
5. Read *Miss Mouse Takes Off*.

6. Time to fly! Give everyone a boarding pass and line them up at "security." As they walk through the security gate, place any "luggage," books, etc., that they could be carrying onto the table as you would for a conveyer. Be sure that the luggage has tags. Check the monitor for departure/arrival times.
7. Let's board! Lead the children through the "terminal" and into the plane. Once everyone is seated, pretend to take off.
8. We're flying! Pretend that the plane is flying. Look out the window. Notice the clouds and bright sun. Watch out for birds!
9. Time to land! Pretend to land the plane. Let everyone exit as they entered. Don't forget to pick up your luggage.
10. Free play! Use the remainder of the time for free play, allowing the children to play as airport employees and passengers.

Final Thoughts

Setting up a pretend airport is a great way to use the imagination and foster the developmental skills children need to grow and learn about the world around them. While learning about airplanes and airports, children will also:
1. Use their imaginations as they explore various ways to play around the pretend airport.
2. Develop thinking skills as they consider what goes on at an airport and use various items such as boxes and tables for other purposes.
3. Enhance language skills by engaging in conversations about airplanes and airports with other children and listening to stories and songs that use specific vocabulary words pertaining to airplanes/airports.
4. Build social skills by sharing props and conversing with other children during airport play.
5. Exercise motor skills as they participate in interactive song and physical play.

Let's Pretend: Pumpkin Patch

Overview

It's pumpkin picking time! Grab your wagons and let's head out to the pumpkin patch. "Let's Pretend: Pumpkin Patch" offers ideas on how to set up a make-believe pumpkin patch using books, songs, props, and pumpkin-related activities.

Materials Needed

Props

Pumpkin Patch: rectangular boxes, crumpled/ shredded newspaper painted brown, orange balloons, fake vine

Fill several small rectangular boxes with the newspaper (dirt). Blow up the balloons and tape the tie part to the vine. Place them in the pumpkin patch (see Figure 26.1).

Scarecrow: newspaper, pants, shirt, boots, hat, pillowcase

Figure 26.1. Let's pick pumpkins!

Stuff the pants, shirt, and pillowcase with newspaper. Tie the pillowcase and tuck it into the neck of the shirt. Tuck the shirt into the pants. Place the boots over the pants leg. Draw a face on the pillowcase and add a hat (see Figure 21.1, p. 58).

Pumpkin Patch Store: box, construction paper

Use a box for a pumpkin patch store. Cut out a window on one side and a door on another. Use construction paper to make a sign.

Coins: cardboard

Cut round pieces out of cardboard and spray paint silver or cover with foil.

Kitchen/Oven: box, caps, foil

Cut an opening in a box to make a door and use as an oven. Cover caps with foil and glue to the oven for knobs.

Pumpkin Pie: recipe, pie pan, construction paper.

Use a recipe to make a pumpkin pie. Cover a pie pan with orange construction paper to make a pretend pie.

Wagon: box, rope, 4 paper plates

Tie a rope to a box to use as a wagon. Paint the paper plates black and glue to the box for wheels (see Figure 26.2).

Books

Serfozo, Mary. *Plumply, Dumply Pumpkin*. New York: Margaret McElderry Books, 2001.

Sloat, Teri. *Patty's Pumpkin Patch*. New York: G. P. Putman's Sons, 1999.

Music

Allard, Peter T., and Ellen Allard. "Hello Everybody." *Sing It! Say It! Stamp It! Sway It! Volume 1* [CD]. Worcester, MA: 80-Z Music, 1999.

Figure 26.2. A wagon to pull the pumpkins!

"The Pumpkin Patch." *Jumpin' in the Leaves* [CD]. Media, PA: Makin' Music Rockin' Rhythms, 1999.

Pumpkin Patch: A Step-by-Step Example Program

1. Opening song: "Hello Everybody."
2. Talk with the children about pumpkin patches. Ask them questions such as:
   - What is a pumpkin patch? (where pumpkins grow)
   - When do you pick pumpkins? (fall)
3. Read *Patty's Pumpkin Patch*.
4. Listen to "The Pumpkin Patch."
5. Read *Plumply, Dumply Pumpkin*.
6. Let's visit the pumpkin patch! Pull the wagon(s) to the pumpkin patch. Let the children examine the pumpkins to determine which ones are "ripe." Let them each choose one to pick and put in the wagon.
7. Time to pay! Pull the wagon over to the store and let each child purchase their pumpkin.
8. Let's cook! Pretend to make a pumpkin pie and place it in the oven. When it's ready take out the real pumpkin pie and enjoy the dessert.
9. Free play! Use the remainder of the time for free play, allowing the children to play or work in the pumpkin patch as they choose.

Final Thoughts

Pretending to be at a pumpkin patch offers a variety of ways to use the imagination for make-believe play and foster the developmental skills children need to grow and learn about the world around them. While learning about pumpkin patches, children will also learn to:

1. Use their imaginations while pretending to be at a pumpkin patch, store, and kitchen.
2. Develop thinking skills as they consider what goes on at a pumpkin patch and use items such as boxes and balloons for various purposes.

3. Enhance language skills as they listen to stories, songs, and poems about pumpkins and engage in pretend play.
4. Build social skills by learning to share and converse with other children while pretending to pick pumpkins and bake pies.
5. Exercise motor skills as they participate in interactive songs and physical play such as "pumpkin picking."

Let's Pretend: In the Kitchen

Overview

A pretend kitchen is one of the most popular toys that children have. You can create your own by using a few items that are soon to be garbage. "Let's Pretend: In the Kitchen" offers ideas on how to craft a make-believe kitchen and introduce children to kitchen tasks with books, songs, props, and kitchen-related activities.

Materials Needed

Props

Stove: box, paper plates, bottle caps, aluminum foil

Paint the box. Cover the paper plates and bottle caps with aluminum foil. Use the plates as burners and the bottle caps as knobs. Glue them to the box stove. Make an "oven" by cutting a door in the front of the box (see Figure 27.1).

Figure 27.1. Let's cook!

Sink: box, aluminum foil, empty detergent bottle, sponge/dish rag

A small box can be used for a sink, stocked with an empty detergent bottle and a cloth to "wash dishes." Add a faucet by rolling a piece of aluminum foil and curving it at the end. Glue it to the sink box (see Figure 27.2).

Table: children's table or place a blanket/sheet on the floor, construction paper, paper cups/plates/flatware, pictures of food/empty food containers

Figure 27.2. A sink for washing dishes

Set the table with construction paper placemats, paper plates and cups, flatware, centerpiece, and pictures of food/empty food containers for pretend eating.

Miscellaneous: pots, pans, non-sharp utensils, oven mitts

Books

Rockwell, Anne. *Pots and Pans*. New York: Macmillan Publishing Company, 1993.

Music

Allard, Peter T., and Ellen Allard. "Hello Everybody." *Sing It! Say It! Stamp It! Sway It! Volume 1* [CD]. Worcester, MA: 80-Z Music, 1999.

Wiggles. "Hot Potato." *Yummy Yummy* [CD]. Irving, TX: Lyrick Studios, 1999.

In the Kitchen: A Step-by-Step Example Program

1. Opening song: "Hello Everybody."
2. Talk with the children about kitchens. Ask them question such as:
   - What do you find in the kitchen? (stove, food, etc.)
   - What do you do in the kitchen? (prepare food, eat, etc.)
3. Read *Pots and Pans*.
4. Use food props and listen to "Hot Potato."
5. Let's prepare a meal. Show the children how to use the props to make a pretend meal.
6. Time to eat! Help the children set the table(s). Enjoy the pretend meal.
7. Cleanup time! Show them how to clean up after the meal. Clear the tables, wash the dishes, and put them away.
8. Free play! Use the remainder of the time for free play, allowing the children to prepare meals and eat as they choose.

Final Thoughts

Creating a pretend kitchen offers children a variety of ways to use their imaginations and foster the developmental skills they need to grow and learn about the world around them. While learning about the kitchen, children will also:

1. Use their imaginations during role-play as they explore kitchen activities by using props such as pretend stoves and food.
2. Develop thinking skills as they consider appropriate kitchen play and use items such as boxes and empty containers for various purposes.
3. Enhance language skills by listening to stories and songs that use specific vocabulary words pertaining to kitchens and foods and by conversing with other children during kitchen play.
4. Build social skills by sharing and interacting with other children through kitchen role-play.
5. Exercise motor skills as they participate in interactive songs and physical play.

Let's Pretend: At the Doctor

Overview

Children love to take on various roles while playing. This type of play makes excellent use of the imagination and helps develop so many other skills as well. Pretending to be a doctor is one of many roles children can imagine themselves to be during play. "Let's Pretend: At the Doctor" offers ideas on how to set up a make-believe doctor's office using books, songs, props, and doctor-related activities.

Materials Needed

Props

Examining Table: table, white sheet
Cover a table with a white sheet.

Bandages: scrap paper, tape
Cut scrap paper into strips to use as bandages. Tape the bandages where needed

Stethoscope: bottle cap, yarn
Make a stethoscope by attaching two ends of yarn to a bottle cap (like a necklace) (see Figure 28.1).

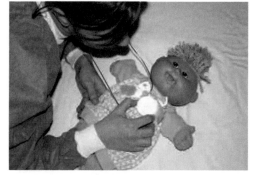

Figure 28.1. Take a deep breath!

Casts: toilet paper roll
Make casts by cutting a slit down a toilet paper roll and write/draw on it as you would decorate a real cast (see Figure 28.2).

Thermometer: drinking straws
Make thermometers by cutting driking straws in half and marking black lines and numbers along the sides.

Tongue Depressors: popsicle sticks

Eye Chart: paper or printed picture

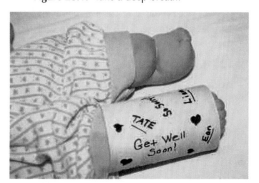

Figure 28.2. A cast for a broken leg

Print an eye chart from the computer or draw one on paper.

X-ray Images: paper or printed picture
Print X-ray images from the computer or draw them on paper.

Syringe (without needle): available at pharmacies

Doctor Bag: old black bag

Dolls

Books

Yolen, Jane. *How Do Dinosaurs Get Well Soon?* New York: Blue Sky Press, 2003.

Music

Allard, Peter T., and Ellen Allard. "Hello Everybody." *Sing It! Say It! Stamp It! Sway It! Volume 1* [CD]. Worcester, MA: 80-Z Music, 1999.

McGrath, Bob, and Katharine Smithrim. "I Went to See My Doctor." *Songs and Games for Toddlers* [CD]. Teaneck, NJ: Bob's Kids Records, 2000.

At the Doctor: A Step-by-Step Example Program

1. Opening song: "Hello Everybody."
2. Talk with the children about the doctor's office. Ask them questions such as:
   - When do you go to the doctor? (checkup, sick, etc.)
   - What happens at the doctor's office? (shots, check temperature, get medicine, etc.)
3. Read *How Do Dinosaurs Get Well Soon?*
4. Listen to "I Went to See My Doctor."
5. We have a sick baby! Take a doll to the doctor's office area and show the children how to use the props to make her feel better.
6. Take her temperature. Explain what the thermometer does, how to use it, and what the marks on the side mean.
7. Give her a shot and tape a bandage to her arm.
8. Look at the X-ray. Does she need a cast? Talk to the children about what a cast is and show them how to put one on the doll's arm.
9. Is she breathing ok? Use the "stethoscope" to check the doll's lungs.
10. Does she have a sore throat? Use the "tongue depressor" to check her throat.
11. How are her eyes? Explain what the eye chart is.
12. Free play! Use the remainder of the time for free play, allowing the children to play in the doctor area as a doctor/nurse, patient, or parent.

Final Thoughts

Setting up a make-believe doctor's office is a great way for children to use their imaginations to try on different roles and to foster the developmental skills they need to grow and learn about the world around them. While learning about doctor's offices and what doctors/nurses do, children also:

1. Use their imaginations as they pretend to be doctors, nurses, patients, and/or parents as they engage in play using props and dialogue.
2. Develop thinking skills as they consider what goes on at a doctor's office and by using items such as boxes, toilet paper rolls, and drinking straws for other purposes.
3. Enhance language skills as they listen to stories and songs/music about the doctor's office and engage in conversation during play.
4. Build social skills as they share props and talk with other children during doctor's office play.
5. Exercise motor skills by participating in interactive songs and through physical play.

Let's Pretend:
A Tea Party

Overview

Tea parties are popular ways to play, especially among girls, and tea sets are classic pretend toys. There are so many different types of tea parties (classic, fairy, teddy bear, royal, etc.). "Let's Pretend: A Tea Party" offers ideas on how to introduce children to a classic style tea party with a story, props, and tea party-related activities.

Materials Needed

Props

Table and Chairs: with tablecloth/picnic blanket/sheet (see Figure 29.1)
Tea Set
Beverages and Food: real or pretend
Napkins
Centerpiece
Dress-up Clothes: hats, scarves, costume jewelry, neckties, etc.

Books

Ichikawa, Satomi. *Nora's Surprise*. New York: Philomel Books, 1994.

Music

Figure 29.1. Let's have tea!

Allard, Peter T., and Ellen Allard. "Hello Everybody." *Sing It! Say It! Stamp It! Sway It! Volume 1* [CD]. Worcester, MA: 80-Z Music, 1999.

Other

"I'm a Little Teapot"

A Tea Party: A Step-by-Step Program Example

1. Opening song: "Hello Everybody."
2. Talk with the children about tea parties. Ask them questions such as:
   • What is a tea party? (friends and fun with tea and desserts)

- What types of tea parties can you have? (classic, royal, fairy, storybook character, etc.)
3. Read *Nora's Surprise.*
4. Sing "I'm a Little Teapot."
5. Tea Manners. Talk to the children about "tea manners."
   - Nothing is served until all guests are seated.
   - Place your spoon on the saucer when you are finished stirring.
   - Put your napkin in your lap.
   - Pat/blot your mouth with your napkin; don't wipe.
   - Always say "please" and "thank you."
6. Let's have tea! Take time to dress for the occasion. Invite everyone to the table(s).
7. Act as the host/hostess and serve everyone a beverage and dessert(s).
8. Encourage table conversation, acting very prim and proper:
   - How delicious is the tea?
   - What is your favorite dessert?
   - Discuss the lovely weather.
9. Free play! Use the remainder of the time for the children to continue with the tea party as they desire.

Final Thoughts

Hosting a pretend tea party is a great way to use the imagination and foster the developmental skills children need to grow and learn about the world around them. While learning about tea parties and etiquette, children will also:

1. Use their imaginations while playing with props such teas sets to create a tea party experience.
2. Develop thinking skills as they participate in activities such as tea etiquette and table conversations.
3. Enhance language skills by listening to a story about a tea party and engaging in tea party conversation.
4. Build social skills by learning to share and converse with other children during tea party play.
5. Exercise motor skills by participating in interactive song and physical play such as pouring and serving.

Let's Pretend: Dance Studio

Overview

A studio is a place where artists work or practice, letting the creativity flow. A dance studio is a place where dancers of all types practice their dance styles. "Let's Pretend: A Dance Studio" offers ideas on how to introduce children to dance and turn your room into a pretend dance studio with books, songs, props, and of course, dancing.

Materials Needed

Props

Scarves

Dance Streamers: crepe paper, paper plate
Cut the crepe paper into strips and glue to one side of the plate. Cut a hole in the other side of the plate for a handle.

Dance Ribbons: ribbons, dowel
Wrap ribbons around the dowel, allowing the ends to hang.

Tap Shoes: cardboard, bottle caps
Cut cardboard to a size slightly bigger than a preschooler's shoe. Glue the rim of the bottle caps (metal preferably) to the bottom for taps. Attach string/yarn or rubber band around the cardboard to hold the cardboard onto the child's shoe. The caps should be flat enough not to damage the floor's surface, but you can also use several large pieces of cardboard as a dance floor.

Ballet Shoes: ribbon
Tie ribbon around feet/ankles to look like ballet/point shoes.

Hula Skirt: paper grocery bag
Cut the bottom out of the bag and a slit down the seam to open it up to one big piece. Cut the bag into strips,

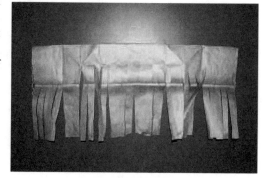

Figure 30.1. Let's hula!

making it like grass, and leave about two inches at the top. Attach a piece of yarn to each end for a tie around the waist (see Figure 30.1).

Dance Posters: Print pictures from the computer or draw some on poster board.

Mirrors: real or pretend (cardboard covered with foil)

Classical Music

Books

Jones, Bill T., and Susan Kuklin. *Dance!* New York: Hyperion Books for Children, 1998.

Schick, Eleanor. *I Am: I Am a Dancer*. New York: Marshall Cavendish, 2002.

Music

Allard, Peter T., and Ellen Allard. "Hello Everybody." *Sing It! Say It! Stamp It! Sway It! Volume 1* [CD]. Worcester, MA: 80-Z Music, 1999.

"Biddy Biddy." *Jumpin' in the Leaves* [CD]. Media, PA: Makin' Music Rockin' Rhythms, 1999.

Gill, Jim. "Silly Dance Contest." *The Sneezing Song and Other Contagious Tunes* [CD]. Chicago: Jim Gill Music, 1993.

"Hukilua." *Folk Dances of Hawaii* [CD]. Miami: Belwin Mills Pub. Corp., 1994.

Litwin, Eric. "The Number Dance." *The Big Silly with Mr. Eric* [CD]. 2006.

Peterson, Carole. "Dancing Scarf Blues." *Dancing Feet* [CD]. 2008.

Dance Studio: A Step-by-Step Program Example

1. Opening song: "Hello Everybody."
2. Talk with the children about dancing and dance studios. Ask them questions such as:
   - What is dancing? (creative movement to music, a way to tell a story, etc.)
   - What types of dancing can you do? (ballet, square, hip-hop, etc.)
   - What is a dance studio? (where you learn and practice dances)
3. Read *I Am: I Am a Dancer*.
4. Dance to "Biddy Biddy."
5. Read *Dance!*
6. Let's explore dancing! Welcome the children to the "studio" and tell them that you will all be doing different types of dancing to different music.
7. First dance: Play "The Number Dance."
8. Next dance: Hand out scarves and play "Dancing Scarf Blues."
9. Third dance: Teach the children how to hula to "Hukilua."
10. Final dance: Play "Silly Dance Contest" to see who can be the silliest dancer.
11. Free play! Use the remainder of the time for free play, allowing the children to try out different props for different dances. Be sure to play a variety of music.

Final Thoughts

Setting up a pretend dance studio generates a lot of opportunity for imaginative play and fosters the developmental skills children need to learn about the world around them. While learning about dancing and dance studios, children will also:

1. Use their imaginations to express themselves with creative dance using music and props.
2. Develop thinking skills as they learn different dance styles and use props for pretend play.
3. Enhance language skills by listening to stories and songs about dancing and by communicating with others during play.
4. Build social skills by sharing props with others and by engaging in social dancing.
5. Exercise motor skills through various dance moves.

Let's Pretend: A Dinosaur Dig

Overview

They were big. They were scary. And they probably walked in your backyard. They're dinosaurs! Maybe we can find some today. "Let's Pretend: A Dinosaur Dig" offers ideas on how to introduce children to dinosaurs and go in search for them, using books, songs, props, and dinosaur-related activities all in a "dinosaur days" setting.

Materials Needed

Props

Jungle Scene: table, green butcher paper, dinosaur pictures

Tape the paper to all sides of the table and shred it to look like grass. Decorate with pictures printed from the computer or drawn on poster board (see Figure 31.1).

Cave: table, sheet, fake plants, dinosaur pictures

Cover a table with a sheet. Cut an opening in the sheet for the entrance. Decorate with fake plants and pictures printed from the computer or drawn on poster board.

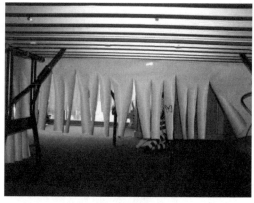

Figure 31.1. Any dinosaurs hiding in this jungle?

Volcano: brown butcher paper, red poster board

Cut a volcano shape out of the butcher paper. Cut lava out of the poster board and tape it to the volcano for an "erupt" effect. Hang the volcano on the wall.

Fossil Dig: several boxes, crumpled/shredded newspaper, popsicle sticks

Fill several boxes with the newspaper (dirt). Hide popsicle sticks throughout the boxes for "bones." Place a box in each area (jungle, cave, volcano).

Dinosaur Skeleton: cardboard, 2 dinosaur pictures

Glue a large dinosaur picture (printed from the computer or made from poster board) on a piece of cardboard. Cut the glued picture into puzzle pieces. Scatter the pieces throughout the dig boxes. Make a copy of the picture to show what the puzzle looks like upon completion. Make several different puzzles.

Dinosaur Eggs: plastic eggs, small plastic dinosaurs

Place dinosaurs in the eggs but leave some eggs empty. Hide the eggs in the boxes and throughout the jungle and cave.

Books

Blackstone, Stella. *I Dreamt I Was a Dinosaur*. Cambridge, MA: Barefoot Books, 2005.

Music

Allard, Peter T., and Ellen Allard. "Hello Everybody." *Sing It! Say It! Stamp It! Sway It! Volume 1* [CD]. Worcester, MA: 80-Z Music, 1999.

Murphy, Jane. "Dinosaur Dance." *Once Upon a Dinosaur* [CD]. Long Branch, NJ: Kimbo Educational, 1987.

Dinosaur Dig: A Step-by-Step Program Example

1. Opening song: "Hello Everybody."
2. Talk with the children about dinosaurs. Ask them questions such as:
   - What are dinosaurs? Name a few.
   - What did they eat?
3. Read *I Dreamt I Was a Dinosaur*.
4. Play/act out "Dinosaur Dance."
5. Let's hunt some dino eggs! Maybe some mothers left some behind. Tell the children to explore the areas to see if they can find any eggs with baby dinosaurs.
6. Let's dig! Show the children the picture of the dinosaur you are looking for. Let them find the pieces and try to put them together. Explain that this is similar to how the giant dinosaur skeletons are found and put together in museums.
7. Free play! After the puzzle is put together, allow the children to use the remainder of the time for free play in the cave, jungle, and digging areas.

Final Thoughts

Setting up a dinosaur dig in a dinosaur days setting allows great opportunity for children to use their imaginations and foster the developmental skills they need to grow and learn about the world around them. While learning about dinosaurs, children will also:

1. Use their imaginations as they play in a "dinosaur days" setting.
2. Develop thinking skills as they search for dinosaurs and put pieces together.
3. Enhance language skills as they listen to stories and songs pertaining to dinosaurs and converse with each other during play.
4. Build social skills as they share props and engage in conversation.
5. Exercise motor skills as they participate in interactive songs and physical play such as digging for "dinosaur remains."

Let's Pretend: At the Park

Overview

National parks, urban parks, bark parks. There is always so much to see and do at parks, even at make-believe parks. "Let's Pretend: At the Park" offers ideas on how to set up a make-believe park using a story, music, props, and park-related activities.

Materials Needed

Props

Picnic Area: blanket, picnic basket, empty food containers, paper plates, cups, flatware

Spread out the blanket for children to sit on and add the different props (see Figure 32.1).

Figure 32.1. A picnic at the park

Pond: blue poster board or butcher paper, construction paper, magnets

Cut a large piece of poster board or butcher paper to look like the shape of a pond. Cut the paper into fish shapes. Glue a magnet on the back of each fish. Place them in the "pond" (see Figure 1.2, p. 1).

Fishing Poles: dowels, string, paper clip

Tie a string around the end of the dowel. Tie a paper clip to the end of the string.

Tackle Box: egg carton, pipe cleaner, paint, paper clips

Paint the egg carton as desired. Poke two holes in the top and insert the pipe cleaner to make a

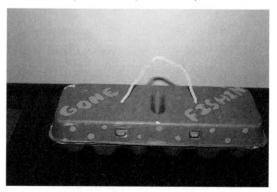

Figure 32.2. Let's fish!

handle. Make knots on each end of the pipe cleaner to keep it from slipping through the holes. Fill the egg carton with paper clips to be used as fishing supplies (see Figure 32.2).

Rubber Ducks: to put in the pond

Puddles: brown butcher paper or poster board

Cut the butcher paper or poster board to look like a mud puddle (see Figure 45.1, p. 119).

Boating Lake: blue poster board or butcher paper, toy boats

Cut a large piece of poster board or butcher paper to look like the shape of a lake. Add toy boats.

Lemonade Stand: table, poster board, pitcher, cups, lemonade

Use the poster board to make a sign. Place a pitcher and cups on the table for easy access. Have ready-made cups if you are working with younger children.

Dog Area: poster board, paper towel rolls, stuffed dogs

Use the poster board to make a "Dog Area" sign. Use paper towel rolls for fetching sticks.

Kites: construction paper, yarn

Draw and cut out diamond shapes on construction paper and attach a piece of yarn to the bottom (see Figure 6.2, p. 17). Decorate as you desire.

Trees: brown and green butcher paper or poster board

Cut the brown paper into tree trunk shapes and the green paper into bushy tree top shapes. Place the green "foliage" at the top of the trunk (see, e.g., Figure 15.1, p. 42). Make various sizes and tape them to the wall.

Pictures of Forest Animals

Binoculars: toilet paper rolls, yarn

Attach yarn to two toilet paper rolls by punching a hole in each roll and making a knot in the yarn to keep it from sliding through the hole (see Figure 16.3, p. 46).

Nature Trail: trees (see above) and forest animal pictures (see above).

Arrange trees along a wall and place the forest animal pictures in various locations. Use the binoculars (see above) to "search" for the animals (see Figure 1.3, p. 2).

Bubbles

Books

Gosney, Joy. *Naughty Parents*. Brookfield, CT: The Millbrook Press, 2000.

Music

Allard, Peter T., and Ellen Allard. "Hello Everybody." *Sing It! Say It! Stamp It! Sway It! Volume 1* [CD]. Worcester, MA: 80-Z Music, 1999.

Parachute Express. "Bubbles." *Feel the Music* [CD]. Glendale, CA: Trio Lane Records, 1998.

At the Park: A Step-by-Step Program Example

1. Opening song: "Hello Everybody."
2. Talk with the children about parks. Ask them questions such as:
   - What types of parks are there? (city park, water park, bark park, etc.)
   - What do you do at parks? (run, fly kites, play ball, etc)
3. Read *Naughty Parents*.
4. Set the mood for fun with bubbles as you play "Bubbles."
5. Let's play! Take the children to each area of the park and show them how to use the props to play.

6. Free play! Use the remainder of the time for free play, allowing the children to play in the different areas with the different props as he/she chooses.

Final Thoughts

Creating a make-believe park offers children numerous ways to use their imaginations and foster the developmental skills they need to grow and learn about the world around them. While pretending to be at a park, children will also:

1. Use their imaginations as they play with props to create a park play experience.
2. Develop thinking skills as they consider the types of activities you can do at a park and by using items such as paper towel rolls and toilet paper rolls for other purposes.
3. Enhance language skills as they listen to a story and songs and converse with other children during park play.
4. Build social skills as they share the park props and engage in conversation.
5. Exercise motor skills as they participate in interactive songs and physical play such as kite-flying and fetching.

Let's Pretend: On Stage

Overview

The stage is ready. The audience is waiting. Whether you're a ballet dancer or a rock star, you're still a performer! "Let's Pretend: On Stage" offers ideas on how to introduce children to various on-stage performances using books, music, props, and activities.

Figure 33.1. Let's make music!

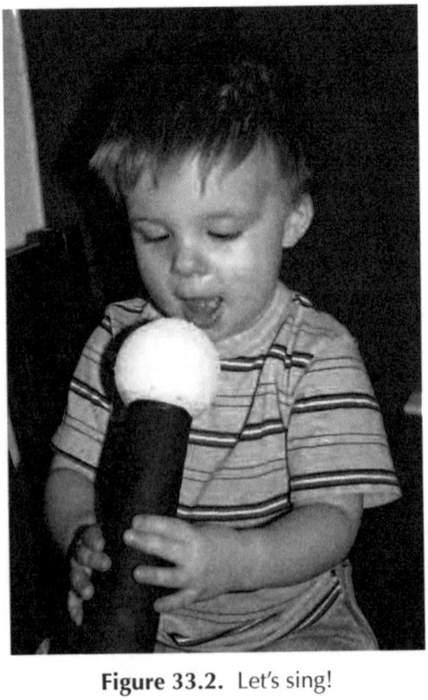

Materials Needed

Props

Stages: tape or 2 carpet pieces/large rugs, 4 coat tree stands, 2 curtains, 2 curtain rods

Place a piece of carpet/large rug on the floor to create a stage area or tape off an area. Use 2 coat tree stands to hold up a curtain rod and hang the curtain on the rod. Make two different stage areas.

Drum Set: plastic containers with lids, 2 dowels, electrical tape

Glue several containers together to make a drum set. Make a ball of tape on the end of the dowel (see Figure 33.1).

Keyboard: rectangular box

Paint the box to look like a keyboard with keys and speakers.

Microphone: paper towel roll, Styrofoam ball

Glue the Styrofoam ball to the end paper towel roll (see Figure 33.2).

Guitar: shoebox, wrapping paper roll, rubber bands

Wrap rubber bands around the shoe box. Glue the wrapping paper roll to one end of the shoe box for a handle.

Dance Streamers: crepe paper, paper plate

Cut the crepe paper into strips and glue to one side of the plate. Cut a hole in the other side of the plate for a handle.

Dance Ribbons: ribbons, dowel

Wrap ribbons around the dowel, allowing the ends to hang.

Figure 33.2. Let's sing!

Tap Shoes: cardboard, bottle caps

Cut cardboard to a size slightly bigger than a preschooler's shoe. Glue the rim of the bottle caps (metal preferably) to the bottom for taps. Attach string/yarn or rubber band around the cardboard to hold the cardboard on to the child's shoe. The caps should be flat enough not to damage the floor's surface, but you can also use several large pieces of cardboard as a dance floor.

Ballet Shoes: ribbon

Tie ribbon around feet/ankles to look like ballet/point shoes.

Puppet Stage: table, bedsheet/blanket

Cover a table with a sheet or blanket.

3 Little Pigs Stick Puppets: popsicle sticks, pictures that go with the story

Print pictures from the computer or draw them on paper and glue to the popsicle sticks.

Various Puppets

Various Types of Music: for playing instruments and dancing

Concession Stand: table, cups, popcorn, beverage

Books

Carlson, Nancy. *Harriet's Recital.* Minneapolis: Carolrhoda Books, Inc., 1982.

Krosoczka, Jarrett. *Punk Farm.* New York: Alfred A. Knopf, 2005.

Music

Allard, Peter T., and Ellen Allard. "Hello Everybody." *Sing It! Say It! Stamp It! Sway It! Volume 1* [CD]. Worcester, MA: 80-Z Music, 1999.

Other

"The Three Little Pigs"

On Stage: A Step-by-Step Program Example

1. Opening song: "Hello Everybody."
2. Talk with the children about stage performances. Ask them questions such as:
   - What are some different types of stage performances? (concerts, plays, recitals, etc.)
   - What are some things that you see on stage? (props, microphones, speakers, etc.)
3. Read *Harriet's Recital.*
4. Use puppets and the puppet stage to present "The Three Little Pigs," encouraging the children to "huff and puff" at the appropriate times.
5. Read *Punk Farm.*
6. Let's put on a music concert! Bring the children to the music concert stage area. Introduce them to the instruments. Play a song from a CD and ask for a few volunteers to join you on stage while the other children act as the audience. Be sure that they visit the concession stand before the show starts!
7. Let's dance! Bring the children to the dance stage. Introduce them to the props. Play a song from a music CD and ask for a few volunteers to join you on stage while the other children act as the audience. Be sure that they visit the concession stand before the show starts.

8. The puppet stage. Show the children the puppet stage and the various props and puppets that can be used for storytelling.
9. Free play! Use the remainder of the time for free play, allowing the children to play on the various stages or act as audience members.

Final Thoughts

Setting up pretend stages generates a lot of opportunity for imaginative play and fosters the developmental skills children need to learn about the world around them. While learning about stage performance, children will also:

1. Use their imaginations to express themselves creatively with various props as they perform.
2. Develop thinking skills as they learn about different types of stage performances and use various items such as paper towel rolls and boxes for other purposes.
3. Enhance language skills by listening to music and stories about performing and by communicating with others during play.
4. Build social skills by sharing props with others and by engaging in pretend play.
5. Exercise motor skills by participating in pretend performances such as dancing.

Let's Pretend: House

Overview

Playing house has always been popular among children and there are elaborate toys on the market catering to this type of role-play. But you don't have to spend a lot of money to create a make-believe house for children to enjoy. "Let's Pretend: House" offers ideas on how to create a pretend house setting using stories, props, and house-related activities.

Materials Needed

Props

Stove: box, paper plates, bottle caps, aluminum foil

> Paint the box. Cover the paper plates and bottle caps with aluminum foil. Use the plates as burners and the bottle caps as knobs. Glue them to the box stove. Make an "oven" by cutting a door in the front of the box (see Figure 34.1).

Sink: box, aluminum foil, empty detergent bottle, sponge/dish rag

> A small box can be used for a sink, stocked with an empty detergent bottle and a cloth to "wash dishes." Add a faucet by rolling a piece of aluminum foil and curving it at the end. Glue it to the sink box (see Figure 34.2).

Table: children's table or place a blanket/sheet on the floor, construction paper, paper cups/plates/flatware, pictures of food/empty food containers

> Set the table with construction paper placemats, paper plates and cups, flatware, centerpiece, and pictures of food/empty food containers for pretend eating.

Figure 34.1. Let's cook!

Figure 34.2. Let's wash the dishes!

Television: box, pictures, Velcro, cap

> Paint the box black or gray. Cover a cap with aluminum foil and glue to the box as a knob. Print pictures from the computer or draw some on poster board. Use

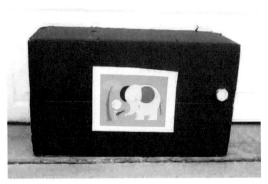

Figure 34.3. TV time!

Velcro to attach the pictures to the box so that you can change them out, as in "changing channels" (see Figure 34.3).

Pet Bed: basket, blanket, stuffed dog and/or cat

Place a blanket in the basket and top it with a dog or cat.

3 Little Pigs Stick Puppets: popsicle sticks, pictures that go with the story

Print pictures from the computer or draw them on paper and glue to the popsicle sticks.

Miscellaneous: pots, pans, non-sharp cooking utensils, broom, feather duster

Books

Tseng, Kevin. *Ned's New Home*. Berkeley, CA: Tricycle Press, 2009.

Wallace, Nancy. *Alphabet House*. Tarrytown, NY: Marshall Cavendish Children, 2005.

Music

Allard, Peter T., and Ellen Allard. "Hello Everybody." *Sing It! Say It! Stamp It! Sway It! Volume 1* [CD]. Worcester, MA: 80-Z Music, 1999.

Other

"The Three Little Pigs"

House: A Step-by-Step Program Example

1. Opening song: "Hello Everybody."
2. Talk with the children about houses/homes. Ask them questions such as:
   - What types of homes are there? (brick, apartments, big, small, animal homes, etc.)
   - What do you find in homes? (kitchen, television, pets, etc.)
   - What are some household chores? (washing dishes, laundry, yard work, etc.)
3. Read *Ned's New Home*.
4. Use puppets to present "The Three Little Pigs." Have the children participate with huffing and blowing.
5. Read *Alphabet House* and ask the children to name the things they see on the pages.
6. Let's play house! Bring the children over to the house area and give them a tour.
7. Let's cook. Show the children how to use the props to make a pretend meal.
8. Time to eat. Help the children set the table(s). Enjoy the pretend meal.
9. Cleanup time! Show them how to clean up after the meal. Clear the table, wash the dishes, and put them away. Then use the broom and feather duster to clean the rest of the house.
10. Let's watch television. Sit them down in front of the television and show them how to change the channels.

11. Free play! Use the remainder of the time for free play, allowing the children to play around the house area as he/she chooses.

Final Thoughts

Creating a make-believe house offers children a lot of ways to use their imagination and foster the developmental skills they need to grow and learn about the world around them. While learning about houses/homes and the roles we participate in while living in houses, children will also:

1. Use their imaginations during role-play as they explore household activities by using props such as pretend stoves, food, and television.
2. Develop thinking skills as they consider appropriate house play and by using items such as boxes and empty containers for various purposes.
3. Enhance language skills by listening to stories about houses and by conversing with other children during house play.
4. Build social skills by sharing and interacting with other children through role-play.
5. Exercise motor skills as they participate in physical play.

Let's Pretend: Art Studio

Overview

Grab your paint, crayons, and play dough and let's make art! "Let's Pretend: Art Studio" shows you how to introduce children to art and encourage their creativity using stories, props, and art-related activities.

Materials Needed

Props

Figure 35.1. Let's paint!

Paint
Pencils, Crayons, and Markers
Play Dough
Glue
Safety Scissors
Construction Paper
Smock: pillowcase
> Cut three holes in the pillowcase along the seam and sides for the head and arms (see Figure 35.1).

Wall Easel: rectangular cardboard piece, paper clip
> Hang cardboard pieces on the wall. Tape/glue a paper clip to the cardboard to hold the "artist's" paper in place (see Figure 35.1).

Models: miscellaneous objects
> Place the objects on the tables for children to use as a guide.

Tables: different one for each medium
> Hang the wall easels by the painting and drawing tables.

Shapes: construction paper
> Make a yellow circle (face), 3 small blue triangles (2 eyes, 1 nose), 1 small rectangle (mouth).

Classical Music
Miscellaneous: buttons, fabric, pipe cleaners, etc.

Books

McDonnell, Patrick. *Art*. New York: Little Brown and Company, 2006.
Whitman, Candace. *Lines That Wiggle*. Maplewood, NJ: Blue Apple Books, 2009.

Music

Allard, Peter T., and Ellen Allard. "Hello Everybody." *Sing It! Say It! Stamp It! Sway It! Volume 1* [CD]. Worcester, MA: 80-Z Music, 1999.

Other

"I'm a Little Artist" (*Tune*: I'm a Little Teapot)

I'm a little artist.
(*Point to self.*)
I like to draw
(*Use finger to draw in the air.*)
And hang my pictures on the wall.
(*Pretend to hang a picture.*)

I can make squares
(*Draw a square in the air.*)
And I can make circles.
(*Draw a circle in the air.*)
I can make them blue
Or another color, maybe purple?

"Little Shapes"

This little circle is yellow.
These little triangles are blue.

This little rectangle is red.
I'll put them together in a picture for you!

Art Studio: A Step-by-Step Example Program

1. Opening song: "Hello Everybody."
2. Talk with the children about art. Ask them questions such as:
   - What are different types of art? (paintings, drawings, etc.)
   - Where is art created? (most of the time in studios)
   - What can be used to create art? (paint, clay, etc.)
3. Read *Art*.
4. Recite "I'm a Little Artist."
5. Read *Lines That Wiggle*.
6. Recite "Little Shapes," using the shapes to create a face.
7. Let's make art! Show the children the different areas to make different things. Play classical music while they work.
8. Show and tell. Let the children show what they have made and tell the others about it.

Final Thoughts

Setting up a place to create artwork generates a lot of opportunity for children to use their imaginations and fosters the developmental skills children need to learn about the world around them. While learning about art, children will also:

1. Use their imaginations to express themselves using various mediums.
2. Develop thinking skills as they ponder what they want to create.
3. Enhance language skills by listening to stories and rhymes about art and by communicating with others during studio play.
4. Build social skills by sharing supplies with others and talking about what they are making.
5. Exercise motor skills as they participate in physical activity such as following "I'm a Little Artist" and using their hands to create artwork.

Let's Pretend: A Dog Show

Overview

Some dogs are small and fluffy. Some dogs are big and scruffy. Some dogs are bad and stay in trouble. Some dogs can do tricks, like catching bubbles. There are all kinds of dogs. "Let's Pretend: A Dog Show" offers ideas on how to introduce children to dogs and their many differences and how to set up a pretend dog show using books, songs, props, and dog-related activities.

Figure 36.1. #1 Doggie

Materials Needed

Props

Stuffed/Plush Dogs: as many as you can get

Paw Prints: black construction paper

Cut paw print shapes out of the construction paper and tape them all over the room.

Grooming Station: table, box, brushes/combs, empty bottles, towels

A small box can be used for a sink, stocked with an empty bottle for shampoo and a towel for drying. Add a faucet by rolling a piece of aluminum foil and curving it at the end. Glue it to the sink box. Place all of the supplies on the table for easy grooming (see Figure 34.2, p. 89).

Stage: tape/carpet piece/large rug

Place a piece of carpet/large rug on the floor to create a stage area or tape off an area.

Fetching Toys: paper towel rolls, cardboard, hula hoop

Use paper towel rolls for fetching sticks. Make Frisbees by cutting out round pieces of cardboard. Use a hula hoop for jumps.

Ruler

Prize Ribbons: construction paper

Cut the paper to look like a winning ribbon (see Figure 36.1).

Books

Hoena, B. A. *Dogs ABC: An Alphabet Book.* Mankato, MN: Capstone Press, 2005.
Saltzberg, Barney. *I Love Dogs.* Cambridge, MA: Candlewick Press, 2005.

Music

Allard, Peter T., and Ellen Allard. "Hello Everybody." *Sing It! Say It! Stamp It! Sway It! Volume 1* [CD]. Worcester, MA: 80-Z Music, 1999.

"Diggin'." *Jumpin' in the Leaves* [CD]. Media, PA: Makin' Music Rockin' Rhythms, 1999.
The Party Cats. "Who Let the Dogs Out?" *Kids Dance Party* [CD]. Brentwood, TN:
Treehouse Entertainment, 2006.

A Dog Show: A Step-by-Step Program Example

1. Opening song: "Hello Everybody."
2. Talk with the children about dogs and dog shows. Ask them questions such as:
   - What are some differences between dogs? (big, small, mean, cuddly)
   - What are dog shows?
3. Read *I Love Dogs*.
4. Listen to/act out "Diggin'"
5. Read *Dogs ABC: An Alphabet Book*.
6. Let's get our dogs ready for the competitions. Give each child a dog to groom at the grooming station.
7. First competition: Smallest Dog. Play "Who Let the Dogs Out?" while the children line up on the stage with their dogs. Use the ruler to determine which dog is the smallest and present a ribbon to the winner.
8. Next competition: Biggest Dog. Play "Who Let the Dogs Out?" while the children line up on the stage with their dogs. Use the ruler to determine which dog is the biggest and present a ribbon to the winner.
9. Third competition: Shortest Tail. Play "Who Let the Dogs Out?" while the children line up on the stage with their dogs. Use the ruler to determine which dog has the shortest tail and present a ribbon to the winner.
10. Fourth competition: Longest Tail. Play "Who Let the Dogs Out?" while the children line up on the stage with their dogs. Use the ruler to determine which dog has the longest tail and present a ribbon to the winner.
11. Last competition: Tricks. Let each child get on stage and use "fetching sticks," Frisbees and/or hula hoops to show off their dog's tricks.
12. Free play! Use the remainder of the time for free play, allowing the children to pretend being contestants, judges, and/or groomers.

Final Thoughts

Setting up a pretend dog show offers children another way to use their imaginations and fosters the developmental skills children need to learn about the world around them. While learning about dogs and dog shows, children will also:

1. Use their imaginations as they play with props such as grooming stations and fetching toys to create a dog show experience.
2. Develop thinking skills as they consider what goes on at a dog show and by determining length and size in the competitions.
3. Enhance language skills as they listen to stories and songs about dogs and by conversing with others during play.
4. Build social skills by sharing and interacting with other children through role-play.
5. Exercise motor skills as they participate in interactive songs and physical play such as pretend dog trick play.

Let's Pretend: A Spring Day

Overview

The snow has melted and the Earth is coming back to life. Let's celebrate the spring season! "Let's Pretend: A Spring Day" offers ideas on how to create a spring day indoors with books, music, props, and spring-related activities.

Materials Needed

Props

Soil: rectangular boxes, crumpled/shredded newspaper painted brown, shredded scrap paper
> Fill several small rectangular boxes with the newspaper (dirt). Use the shredded scrap paper as seeds to plant.

Flower Garden: rectangular boxes, crumpled/shredded newspaper painted brown, construction paper, cardboard
> Fill several small rectangular boxes with newspaper (dirt). Make construction paper flowers and glue them to cardboard for support. Stick the flowers in the "dirt." Spray fragrance on a few. Add paper butterflies and other insects to the area (see Figure 22.1, p. 60).

Watering Can: empty cylinder container (oatmeal container works well), toilet paper roll
> Cut one end of the toilet paper roll at an angle and glue to the container. Paint/decorate as desired.

Kites: construction paper, yarn
> Draw and cut out diamond shapes from construction paper and attach a piece of yarn to the bottom (see Figure 6.2, p. 17). Decorate as you desire.

Tree: branches, flower pot, Styrofoam, brown shredded paper
> Place the branches in the flower pot. Use Styrofoam to make the tree stand. Cover the bottom of the pot with brown shredded paper (dirt).

Bird's Nest and Eggs: straw and/or moss, play dough
> Mold the straw/moss into a bird's nest. Use the play dough to make eggs to put in the nest. Put the nest in the tree.

Bird House/Feeder: milk carton, stick
> Cut an opening on one side of the milk carton for a door. Glue a stick to the opening for a perch. Paint/decorate the house as you desire.

Birds/Butterflies: pictures, pipe cleaners
> Print pictures of birds/butterflies from the computer or make some out of construction paper. Glue a pipe cleaner to the bottom so that you can tie the birds/

butterflies to the tree, flowers, or wear on your finger/wrist (see Figure 37.1).

Bird Food: scrap paper

Clouds: white poster board
Cut various shapes out of the poster board for a cloud picture-guessing activity.

Books

Carr, Jan. *Splish, Splash, Spring.* New York: Holiday House, 2001.

Seuling, Barbara. *Spring Song.* San Diego: Gulliver Books, 2001.

Figure 37.1. A pretty butterfly

Music

Allard, Peter T., and Ellen Allard. "Hello Everybody." *Sing It! Say It! Stamp It! Sway It! Volume 1* [CD]. Worcester, MA: 80-Z Music, 1999.

The Learning Station. "Spring Is Here." *Seasonal Songs in Motion* [CD]. Melbourne, FL: Hug-A-Chug Records, 2001.

A Spring Day: A Step-by-Step Program Example

1. Opening song: "Hello Everybody."
2. Talk with the children about spring. Ask them questions such as:
   - What happens in the spring? (flowers bloom, gets warmer, etc.)
   - What can you do in the spring? (plant gardens, see baby animals, etc.)
3. Read *Spring Song.*
4. Listen/dance to "Spring Is Here."
5. Read *Splish, Splash, Spring.*
6. Let's find shapes in the clouds! Tell the children to lie on their backs and look at the "sky." Walk around and hold the cloud shapes over their heads and let them guess the shapes.
7. Time to plant the garden. Give the children "seeds" and show them how to plant them in the "soil."
8. Stop to smell the blooming flowers! Let the children smell the flowers and try to find the fragrant ones. Then show them how to pick and replant them. Admire the butterflies while you are there and show them how they can "sit" on your wrist.
9. Let's feed the birds! Give them each some "bird food" to put in the birdhouse. Admire the bird while you are there and show them how the birds can "sit" on your finger/wrist.
10. Who wants to fly a kite? Let the children make a kite or give them premade ones to fly around the room.
11. Free play! Use the remainder of the time for free play, allowing the children to enjoy this spring day as they choose.

Final Thoughts

Creating a spring day indoors generates a lot of opportunity for imaginative play and fosters the developmental skills children need to learn about the world around them. While learning about spring and the activities they can participate in during the spring season, children will also:

1. Use their imaginations to engage in pretend spring play by using props such as gardens, birds, butterflies, and kites.
2. Develop thinking skills as they consider what happens in spring while using props to create a spring experience.
3. Enhance language skills by listening to stories and songs about spring and by communicating with others during make-believe spring play.
4. Build social skills by sharing props with others and by engaging in imaginative play.
5. Exercise motor skills by participating in interactive songs and physical play such as "kite flying."

Let's Pretend: In the Mountains

Overview

Caves, hills, and hiking trails are just a few things that make the mountains a fun place to visit and explore. "Let's Pretend: In the Mountains" offers ideas on how to set up a make-believe trip to the mountains using books, songs, props, and mountain-related activities.

Materials Needed

Props

Mountain Backdrop: green or brown butcher paper
> Cut mountain shapes out of the butcher paper and tape to the walls.

Nature Trail: brown and green butcher paper or poster board, picture of forest animals
> Cut the brown paper into tree trunk shapes and the green paper into bushy treetop shapes. Place the green "foliage" at the top of the trunk. Make various sizes and tape them to the wall. Add pictures of forest animals (see Figure 38.1).

Mountains: boxes, tables, and other furniture, green or brown bedsheets
> Cover stacked boxes and furniture with the bedsheets to make mountains. Place them along with the backdrop and nature trail but allow space between the wall and the furniture for walking to create a feel that the children are walking in the mountains.

Figure 38.1. Let's hike!

Cave: table, sheet, bear
> Cover a table with a sheet. Cut an opening in the sheet for the entrance. Place a sleeping bear inside.

Stream: blue butcher paper
> Cut the butcher paper to look like a stream.

Fish: construction paper and magnets
> Cut the paper into fish shapes. Glue a magnet on the back of each fish. Place them in the stream.

Fishing Poles: dowels, string, paper clip
> Tie a string around the end of the dowel. Tie a paperclip to the end of the string.

Berry Bushes: fake plants, red construction paper

Cut round berries out of the construction paper and tape them to the fake plants. Place throughout the mountain area.

Binoculars: toilet paper rolls, yarn

Attach yarn to two toilet paper rolls by punching a hole in each roll and making a knot in the yarn to keep it from sliding through the hole (see Figure 16.3, p. 46).

Basket(s)

Books

Agell, Charlotte. *Up the Mountain*. New York: Dorling Kindersley Publishing, Inc., 2000.

Huneck, Stephen. *Sally Goes to the Mountains*. New York: Harry N. Abrams, Inc., Publishers, 2001.

Music

Allard, Peter T., and Ellen Allard. "Hello Everybody." *Sing It! Say It! Stamp It! Sway It! Volume 1* [CD]. Worcester, MA: 80-Z Music, 1999.

Other

"The Bear Went Over the Mountain"

In the Mountains: A Step-by-Step Program Example

1. Opening song: "Hello Everybody."
2. Talk with the children about mountains. Ask them questions such as:
   • What can you do in the mountains? (hike, ski, etc.)
   • What are some things you see in the mountains? (animals, caves, etc.)
3. Read *Sally Goes to the Mountains.*
4. Sing "The Bear Went Over the Mountain."
5. Read *Up the Mountain.*
6. Let's explore the mountains. Give everyone a set of binoculars and head over to the mountain area.
7. Let's hike. Take the children around the mountains and down the nature trail. Use the binoculars to look for animals.
8. A cave! Take the children into the cave to find the sleeping bear.
9. Let's go berry-picking. Give them baskets and let them find the berry bushes to pick.
10. Time to fish! Let them take turns catching fish in the stream.
11. Free play! Use the remainder of the time for free play, allowing the children to explore the mountains as they choose.

Final Thoughts

Setting up a pretend mountain trip is a great way to use the imagination and foster the developmental skills children need to grow and learn about the world around them. While learning about camping and other outdoor activities, children will also:

1. Use their imaginations while playing with props such as pretend caves and nature trails to create a mountain experience.

2. Develop thinking skills as they participate in activities such as searching for animals on the "nature trail" and by using objects such as sheets and furniture for other purposes.
3. Enhance language skills by listening to stories and songs about the mountains and by engaging in conversation during mountain play.
4. Build social skills by learning to share and converse with other children while pretending to explore the mountains.
5. Exercise motor skills as they participate in interactive songs and physical play such as "hiking."

Let's Pretend: Pizza Parlor

Overview

Yummy, yummy, yummy! It's pizza time! "Let's Pretend: Pizza Parlor" offers ideas on how to set up a pretend pizza parlor and show children how to make a pizza using books, song, props, and pizza-related activities.

Figure 39.1. A yummy play dough pizza

Materials Needed

Props

Tables

Red Tablecloths: real or butcher paper

Cardboard/Play Dough Pizza: cardboard, construction paper, or play dough

Cut out a circle from the cardboard for crust or use white play dough. Use red construction paper or play dough to make sauce and pepperoni. Use white shredded construction paper or play dough pieces for cheese. Use green and black construction paper or play dough for peppers and olives. Layer the "ingredients" on the "crust." Cut slices (see Figure 39.1).

Apron: paper grocery bag

Open the bag's seam and spread it flat. Cut out the bottom. Cut the bag into an apron shape. Punch two holes at the top of the apron and tie a piece of yarn through each to make tie to go around the neck. Punch two more holes at the back of the waist and tie a piece of yarn through each to go around the waist (see Figure 41.2, p. 107).

Pizza Preparation Table: to hold all pizza-making supplies

Miscellaneous: pizza pan, spatula, paper plates, pizza posters

Books

Steig, William. *Pete's a Pizza*. New York: HarperCollins Publishers, 1998.
Wellington, Monica. *Pizza at Sally's*. New York: Dutton Children's Books, 2006.

Music

Allard, Peter T., and Ellen Allard. "Hello Everybody." *Sing It! Say It! Stamp It! Sway It! Volume 1* [CD]. Worcester, MA: 80-Z Music, 1999.
Galipeau, Ken. "I Am a Pizza." *Fishin' with Ish* [CD]. Rockaway, NJ: Story N Song Records, 2005.
Yosi. "It's a Pizza." *What's Eatin' Yosi?* [CD]. Island Heights, NJ: Yosi Music, 2006.

Pizza Parlor: A Step-by-Step Program Example

1. Opening song: "Hello Everybody."
2. Talk to the children about pizza. Ask them questions such as:
   - How do you make a pizza? (roll dough, add topping, etc.)
   - What can you put on pizza? (pepperoni, pineapple, cheese, etc.)
3. Read *Pizza at Sally's*.
4. Use props (flannel board works well) and listen to "I Am a Pizza."
5. Read *Pete's a Pizza*.
6. Pizza Parlor time! Let everyone take a seat at a table and welcome them to your restaurant. Play "It's a Pizza" as you prepare and serve pizza to your guests.
7. Let's make pizza! Gather everyone around the pizza preparation table, give them an apron and show them how to use the props to make a pizza.
8. Free play! Use the remainder of the time for free play, allowing the children to play in the pizza parlor as they wish.

Final Thoughts

Setting up a pretend pizza parlor is a great way to use the imagination and foster the developmental skills children need to grow and learn about the world around them. While learning about making and serving pizza, children will also:

1. Use their imaginations while playing with props such as pretend pizza toppings and aprons to create a pizza parlor experience.
2. Develop thinking skills as they participate in activities such as pizza-making and use materials such as play dough and/or construction paper for various props.
3. Enhance language skills by listening to stories and songs about pizza and by engaging in conversation during pizza parlor play.
4. Build social skills by learning to share and converse with other children while pretending to dine or work in a pizza parlor.
5. Exercise motor skills as they participate in interactive songs and physical play such as making and serving pizza.

Let's Pretend: In the Land of Mother Goose

Overview

So many children grow up learning and reciting nursery rhymes. Make these rhymes even more exciting for children by bringing them to life during play. "Let's Pretend: In the Land of Mother Goose" offers ideas on how to encourage imaginative play using books, music, props, and activities based on these classic rhymes.

Figure 40.1. Jack jumped over the candlestick!

Figure 40.2. He put her in a pumpkin shell and there he kept her very well!

Materials Needed

Props

Humpty Dumpty: building blocks, eggs, pan
> Build a wall with the building blocks. Use a pan to catch the eggs.

Little Miss Muffet: box, chair, fishing line, toy spider, doll
> Cut the top off of the box. Seat the doll on the chair inside the box. Hang the spider on a fishing line and dangle it from the top of the box.

Jack's Candlestick: tall snack food can with plastic lid (Pringles works well), orange construction paper, paint
> Paint the can. Cut a slit in the lid and insert the flame made from construction paper (see Figure 40.1).

Peter Pumpkin Eater's Pumpkin: paper bag, paint, green ribbon, picture of a lady, popsicle stick, bottle cap
> Cut an opening in the front of the bag to make a door. Gather the bag at the top and tie it with the ribbon. Paint the bag orange to look like a pumpkin. Glue a picture of a lady to a popsicle stick and glue the popsicle stick to the bottle cap to make the lady stand. Place her inside the pumpkin's door (see Figure 40.2).

Hickory Dickory Dock: paper plate, construction paper, brad, electrical tape
> Write numbers around the edge of the plate. Make two clock hands out of construction paper and

attach them to the plate using a brad. Use electrical tape to make a lane big enough for the children to crawl down.

Contrary Mary's Garden: rectangular box, crumpled/shredded newspaper painted brown, construction paper, cardboard

Fill the rectangular box with the newspaper (dirt). Make construction paper flowers that go with the rhyme and glue them to cardboard for support. Stick the flowers in the "dirt." Spray fragrance on a few. Add paper butterflies and other insects to the area (see Figure 22.1, p. 60).

Twinkle, Twinkle, Little Star: box (big enough for a child to sit in), flashlight, construction paper

Paint the box black. Poke small holes in the shape of a star into a piece of black construction paper and fit it over a flashlight.

Books

Edwards, Pamela Duncan. *The Neat Line: Scribbling through Mother Goose*. New York: Katherine Tegen Books, 2005.

Jackson, Alison. *If the Shoe Fits*. New York: Henry Holt and Company, 2001.

Music

Allard, Peter T., and Ellen Allard. "Hello Everybody." *Sing It! Say It! Stamp It! Sway It! Volume 1* [CD]. Worcester, MA: 80-Z Music, 1999.

Levy, Micah. "Humpty Dumpty" (Rock and Roll) and "Little Miss Muffet" (Romantic). *Mother Goose and Her Fabulous Puppet Friends* [CD]. Diane Ligon, 2008.

Other

"Jack, Be Nimble"
"London Bridge"
"Peter, Peter, Pumpkin Eater"
"Hickory Dickory Dock"
"Mary, Mary, Quite Contrary"
"Twinkle, Twinkle, Little Star"

In the Land of Mother Goose: A Step-by-Step Program Example

1. Opening song: "Hello Everybody."
2. Talk with the children about Mother Goose rhymes. Ask them questions such as:
   - What is their favorite rhyme?
   - How would they like to live in the land of Mother Goose?
3. Read *If the Shoe Fits*.
4. Use props as you listen to "Humpty Dumpty."
5. Read *The Neat Line: Scribbling through Mother Goose*.
6. Use props as you listen to "Little Miss Muffet."
7. "Jack, Be Nimble": Line the children up and recite "Jack, Be Nimble" (substituting each child's name for "Jack") as they take turns jumping over the candlestick.
8. "London Bridge": Tell the children to form two lines facing each other and hold hands up high, forming a bridge, with the person they are facing. Recite

"London Bridge," letting each child have a turn walking down the bridge until one gets caught (the children bring their arms down to catch the person).

9. Use the prop and recite "Peter, Peter, Pumpkin Eater."
10. "Hickory Dickory Dock": Place the clock on the floor and form a lane. Recite "Hickory Dickory Dock," letting one child at a time crawl down the lane to the clock, pretending to be the mouse.
11. "Mary, Mary, Quite Contrary": Bring the children to the garden and recite "Mary, Mary, Quite Contrary."
12. "Twinkle, Twinkle, Little Star": Turn the lights down and use the starmaker while reciting "Twinkle, Twinkle, Little Star." The children can use the box during free play.
13. Free play! Use the remainder of the time for free play, allowing the children to explore the Land of Mother Goose as they choose.

Final Thoughts

Bringing nursery rhymes to life offers children a variety of ways to use their imaginations and foster the developmental skills they need to grow and learn about the world around them. While learning and acting out nursery rhymes, the children will also:

1. Use their imaginations while using nursery rhyme props.
2. Develop thinking skills as they consider nursery rhyme verses and use props for various purposes.
3. Enhance language skills as they listen to stories and songs, recite nursery rhymes and converse with others.
4. Build social skills as they share props, such as the starmaker, and engage in conversation during play.
5. Exercise motor skills as they participate in interactive songs and physical play such as jumping over candlesticks and crawling like a mouse.

Let's Pretend:
At the Bakery

Overview

Yummy treats and tasty sweets…there are lots of good things to bake and eat at the bakery. "Let's Pretend: At the Bakery" offers ideas on how to set up a pretend bakery for eating and baking with a story, music, props, and bakery-related activities.

Materials Needed

Props

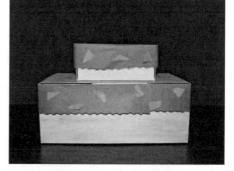

Figure 41.1. A yummy cake

Cake: 2 or more boxes, paint, construction paper
Paint the boxes and stack them on top of each other for layers. Use construction paper to decorate the cake (see Figure 41.1).
Pie: pie pan, play dough
Fill the pie pan with play dough.
Cookies: play dough, cookie cutters
Use cookie cutters to cut cookies out of the play dough.
Food: empty containers and/or boxes with labels glued to them
Stove/Oven: box, paper plates, bottle caps, aluminum foil
Paint the box. Cover the paper plates and bottle caps with aluminum foil. Use the plates as burners and the bottle caps as knobs. Glue them to the box stove. Make an "oven" by cutting a door in the front of the box (see Figure 34.1, p. 89).
Apron: paper grocery bag
Open the bag's seam and spread it flat. Cut the bag into an apron shape. Punch two holes at the top of the apron and tie a piece of yarn through each to make tie to go around the neck. Punch two more holes at the back of the waist and tie a piece of yarn through each to go around the waist (see Figure 41.2).

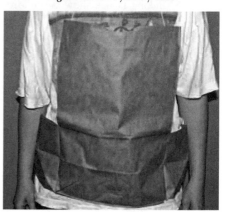

Figure 41.2. Ready to bake!

Tables: one for each different activity
Use some tables to prepare food, some to display food for sale, and some to sit at and eat.

Register: box, green and gray construction paper

Make bills out of green construction paper and coins out of gray construction paper. Use the box as a register.

Real Cakes, Cookies, and/or Pie

Miscellaneous: doilies, paper plates, mixing bowls, spoons, pan, rolling pin, baking sheet

Books

Andreasen, Dan. *The Baker's Dozen*. New York: Henry Holt and Company, 2007.

Music

Allard, Peter T., and Ellen Allard. "Hello Everybody." *Sing It! Say It! Stamp It! Sway It! Volume 1* [CD]. Worcester, MA: 80-Z Music, 1999.

Wiggles. "Crunchy Munchy Honey Cakes." *Yummy Yummy* [CD]. Irving TX: Lyrick Studios, 1999.

At the Bakery: A Step-by-Step Program Example

1. Opening song: "Hello Everybody."
2. Talk with the children about bakeries. Ask them questions such as:
   • What do you do at a bakery? (buy sweets, eat, bake, etc.)
   • What are some things made at a bakery? (cookies, cakes, etc.)
3. Read *The Baker's Dozen*.
4. Use props and listen to "Crunchy Munchy Honey Cakes."
5. Let's go to the bakery! Give everyone an apron and lead them to the bakery area.
6. Baking a cake: Show the children how to make a cake by "mixing the ingredients" and then arranging the boxes and decorating it with construction paper cutouts.
7. Baking a pie: Show the children how to bake a pie by "mixing the ingredients," filling the pie pan with play dough, and placing it in the oven.
8. Baking cookies: Show the children how to make cookies by "mixing the ingredients," rolling out the play dough, cutting out the cookies with the cookie cutters, and placing them on a sheet in the oven.
9. Let's eat! Let everyone purchase a slice of cake, pie, or cookie and take a seat to enjoy the tasty treats, which have become real food to eat!
10. Free play! Use the remainder of the time for free play, allowing the children to bake, purchase, and eat the sweet treats as they wish.

Final Thoughts

Setting up a pretend bakery is a great way to use the imagination and foster the developmental skills children need to grow and learn about the world around them. While learning about bakeries and baking, children will also:

1. Use their imaginations while playing with props such as pretend food and aprons to create a bakery experience.
2. Develop thinking skills as they participate in activities such as pretend baking and using materials such as play dough and/or construction paper for various props.

3. Enhance language skills by listening to a story and music about baking and by engaging in conversation during bakery play.
4. Build social skills by learning to share and converse with other children while pretending to eat or work in a bakery.
5. Exercise motor skills as they participate in interactive songs and physical play such as making bakery goodies.

Let's Pretend: At the Pond

Overview

Croaking frogs, chirping crickets, quacking ducks. Ponds are full of life! "Let's Pretend: At the Pond" offers ideas on how to introduce children to pond life with books, music, props, and pond-related activities.

Figure 42.1. Quack, quack!

Figure 42.2. A turtle for the pond

Materials Needed

Props

Pond: large blue tarp
Duck: paper plate, construction paper, popsicle stick

> Cut out two drawings of your hand and a circle from a piece of construction paper. Make a face on the construction paper and add an orange triangle for a bill. Fold the paper plate in half and turn it curved-side down. Glue the circle to one end of the plate and glue mirrored hands to the other end for feathers. Place a popsicle stick flat and glue it to the curved bottom to make the duck stand (see Figure 42.1).

Turtle: paper plate, construction paper

> Color/paint the plate green and cut out four legs and a head from the construction paper. Glue the head and legs to the plate (see Figure 42.2).

Frog: paper plate, construction paper

Color/paint the paper plate green and fold it in half. Cut frog legs out of the construction paper and glue to the paper plate. Add two big eyes and a tongue to the plate.

Lily Pads: construction paper

Cut lily pad shapes out of construction paper and place them in the pond.

Trees: brown and green butcher paper or poster board

Cut the brown paper into tree trunk shapes and the green paper into bushy tree top shapes. Place the green "foliage" at the top of the trunk (see, e.g., Figure 15.1, p. 42). Make various sizes and tape them to the wall.

Cattails: construction paper

Cut the shapes out of construction paper and tape them to the walls with the trees.

Beaver Dam: paper towel rolls

Glue paper towel rolls together to make a dam. Place it in the middle of the pond.

Binoculars: toilet paper rolls, yarn

Attach yarn to two toilet paper rolls by punching a hole in each roll and making a knot in the yarn to keep it from sliding through the hole (see Figure 16.3, p. 46).

Fish: construction paper and magnets

Cut the paper into fish shapes. Glue a magnet on the back of each fish. Place them in the "pond."

Fishing Poles: dowels, string, paper clip

Tie a string around the end of the dowel. Tie a paperclip to the end of the string.

Nature Music

Bread: pieces of scrap paper

Books

Fleming, Denise. *In the Small, Small Pond*. New York: Henry Holt and Company, 1993.

Jordan, Sandra. *Frog Hunt*. Brookfield, CT: Roaring Brook Press, 2002.

Music

Allard, Peter T., and Ellen Allard. "Hello Everybody." *Sing It! Say It! Stamp It! Sway It! Volume 1* [CD]. Worcester, MA: 80-Z Music, 1999.

Moo, Anna. "Five Frogs." *Anna Moo Crackers* [CD]. Newberry, FL: Good Moo's Productions, 1994.

At the Pond: A Step-by-Step Program Example

1. Opening song: "Hello Everybody."
2. Talk with the children about pond life. Ask them questions such as:
   - What do you see at a pond? (frogs, insects, lily pads, etc.)
   - What are some possible sounds? (frogs croaking, crickets chirping, ducks quacking, etc.)
3. Read *Frog Hunt*.
4. Listen to/act out "Five Frogs."
5. Read *In the Small, Small Pond*.
6. Let's visit the pond. Play nature sounds, give the children binoculars and bread and lead them to the pond.
7. Let's feed the ducks. Let the children throw "bread" into the "pond."
8. Let's observe the pond life. Use the binoculars and talk about what you see.
9. Free play! Use the remainder of the time for free play, allowing the children to explore the pond as they choose, building beaver dams, feeding the ducks, etc.

Final Thoughts

Setting up a pretend pond is a great way to use the imagination and foster the developmental skills children need to grow and learn about the world around them. While learning about pond life, children will also:

1. Use their imaginations while playing with props such as pretend binoculars and food to create a pond experience.
2. Develop thinking skills as they participate in activities such as pretend nature-watching and using materials such as toilet paper and paper towel rolls for other purposes.
3. Enhance language skills by listening to stories and music about ponds and by engaging in conversation during pond play.
4. Build social skills by learning to share and converse with other children while pretending to play around the pond.
5. Exercise motor skills as they participate in interactive songs and physical play such as nature watching.

Let's Pretend:
At the Racetrack

Overview

On your mark. Get set. Go! Off to the finish line! Races of all sorts generate a lot of excitement. "Let's Pretend: At the Racetrack" offers ideas on how to introduce children to racetracks using a story, rhymes, props, and race-related activities.

Materials Needed

Props

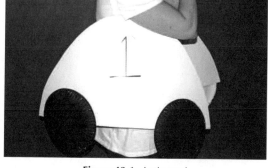

Figure 43.1. Let's race!

Racetrack: electrical tape
Tape lanes on the floor to create a race track. Make more than one track if you have room.

Flags: construction paper, dowels
Make various racing flags out of construction paper and tape to dowels.

Car: 2 poster boards, 4 paper plates, yarn
Cut the shape of a car out of two poster boards. Paint the plates black and glue to the car for wheels. Attach a yarn loop to the top of each to wear over the shoulders (see Figure 43.1).

Horse: 2 poster boards, yarn
Cut the shape of a horse out of two poster boards. Attach a yarn loop to the top of each to wear over the shoulders.

Trophy: small rectangular box
Paint the box gold or silver and add glitter.

Books

Floca, Brian. *The Racecar Alphabet*. New York: Atheneum Books for Young Readers, 2003.

Music

Allard, Peter T., and Ellen Allard. "Hello Everybody." *Sing It! Say It! Stamp It! Sway It! Volume 1* [CD]. Worcester, MA: 80-Z Music, 1999.

Other

"This Little Racecar" (*Tune*: "This Little Piggy")

This little racecar went backwards.
(*Walk backwards.*)
This little racecar went too slow.
(*Move slowly.*)
This little racecar got 2nd place.
(*Hold up 2 fingers.*)
This little racecar got none.
(*Make a sad face.*)
This little racecar went the fastest all the way to the finish line
And he won!
(*Race around the room.*)

"If You're a Racecar and You Know It" (*Tune*: "If You're Happy and You Know It")

If you're a racecar and you know it start your engine.
(*Vroom, vroom*)
If you're a racecar and you know it start your engine.
(*Vroom, vroom*)
If you're a racecar and you know it and you really want to show it
If you're a racecar and you know it start your engine.
(*Vroom, vroom*)

Continue with:

If you're a racecar and you know it beep your horn.
(*Beep, beep*)...
If you're a racecar and you know it steer your wheels.
(*Pretend to turn a steering wheel.*)...
If you're a racecar and you know it go real fast.
(*Race around the room.*)...

At the Race Track: A Step-by-Step Program Example

1. Opening song: "Hello Everybody."
2. Talk with the children about racing/racetracks. Ask them question such as:
   - What types of race tracks are there? (cars, horses, etc.)
   - What do you hear at race tracks? (engines, announcers, etc.)
3. Read *The Racecar Alphabet*.
4. Recite "This Little Racecar."
5. Recite "If You're a Racecar and You Know It."
6. Let's race! Show the children the racetrack and explain what the flags mean. Then line up the ones who want to race and let the others act as spectators. Have a car race first. Then switch to a horserace. Be sure to present a trophy to the winners!
7. Free play! Use the remainder of the time for free play, allowing the children to race or spectate as they wish.

Final Thoughts

Setting up a pretend racetrack is a great way to use the imagination and foster the developmental skills children need to grow and learn about the world around them. While learning about racing, children will also:

1. Use their imaginations while playing with props such as pretend race cars and horses to create a racing experience.
2. Develop thinking skills as they participate in activities such a learning what the race flags mean and using props to play.
3. Enhance language skills by listening to story rhymes about racing and by engaging in conversation during racetrack play.
4. Build social skills by learning to share and converse with other children while pretending to race or act as spectators.
5. Exercise motor skills as they participate in interactive songs and physical play such as racing.

Let's Pretend: In Storybook Land

Overview

Reading a story is a great way to use your imagination to visit other places. But what about actually playing in those faraway lands? "Let's Pretend: In Storybook Land" offers ideas on how to use books, an interactive story, props, and storybook-related activities to create an imaginary world based on people and places we read about in books.

Figure 44.1. Rapunzel, Rapunzel, let down your hair!

Materials Needed

Props

Three Little Pigs: hay/straw, popsicle sticks, building blocks, paper plate/construction paper, paper cup, pipe cleaner, string

Use the hay/straw, popsicle sticks, and building blocks to make houses for the three little pigs. Make a wolf mask by using gray construction paper or coloring a paper plate gray. Cut out two eye holes and glue a black-colored cup to the mask for a nose. Cut out two triangular shapes for ears and glue to the top of the mask. Punch holes on each side of the mask and tie the string through each in order to make the mask wearable.

Goldilocks and the Three Bears: 3 chairs, table, 3 bowls with spoons, sheet, 3 pillows (vary the sizes of these items if possible)

Place the three bowls on a table. Place the three chairs beside each other. Place a sheet on the floor with three pillows to make three beds.

Cinderella: variety of shoes, including one "glass slipper" (clear shoe)

Place the shoes in a pile.

Rapunzel: box, yarn, Velcro, full-length picture of a prince

Paint the box to look like a tower and cut out a window on the front. Braid the yarn and attach it to the box, hanging it out the window. Print a picture of a prince from the computer and apply Velcro to the picture, allowing the prince to "climb" the braid (see Figure 44.1).

Three Billy Goats Gruff: cardboard piece, paper bag

Paint a large piece of cardboard to look like a wooden bridge. Use a paper bag to make an ugly troll mask.

Books

Kloske, Geoffrey, and Barry Blitt. *Once Upon a Time, the End (Asleep in 60 Seconds)*. New York: Antheneum Books for Young Readers, 2005.

Sperring, Mark. *The Fairytale Cake*. New York: Scholastic, Inc., 2005.

Music

Allard, Peter T., and Ellen Allard. "Hello Everybody." *Sing It! Say It! Stamp It! Sway It! Volume 1* [CD]. Worcester, MA: 80-Z Music, 1999.

Other

"Five Little Gingerbread Men"

Five little gingerbread men on the tray,
One jumped up and ran away.
Try to catch me if you can!
I'm a fast little gingerbread man!

Four little gingerbread men on the tray,
One jumped up and ran away.
Try to catch me if you can!
I'm a fast little gingerbread man!

(*Continue until all the gingerbread men are gone.*)

No little gingerbread men on the tray
They were all too fast to catch today!

The Setup: A Step-by-Step Program Example

1. Opening song: "Hello Everybody."
2. Talk with the children about different storybook places and characters. Ask them questions such as:
   - What might you see in a storybook land? (castles, talking animals, etc.)
   - What are some things you might do in a storybook land? (fight dragons, save princesses, etc.)
3. Read *Once Upon a Time, the End (Asleep in 60 Seconds)*. Read only parts of the book if you have very young children.
4. Talk to the children about the story "The Gingerbread Boy." Invite them to join you in reciting "Five Little Gingerbread Men."
5. Read *The Fairytale Cake*.
6. Let's go to storybook land! Tell the children to spin around three times.
7. First stop: The Three Little Pigs. Talk about the story. Then show them how to build a straw house, a stick house, and a brick house. Wear the mask and blow the first two down, encouraging them to "huff and puff" with you.
8. Next stop: Goldilocks and the Three Bears. Talk about the story. Then pretend to be Goldilocks and try out the "porridge," the chairs, and the beds, encouraging

the children to help you decide if they are too hot/cold, big/little, hard/soft, or just right.

9. Third stop: Cinderella. Talk about the story. Then pretend to be Cinderella and try on the different shoes.

10. Fourth stop: Rapunzel. Talk about the story. Then show the children how to make the prince climb her braid.

11. Last stop: Three Billy Goats Gruff. Talk about the story. Then let a volunteer wear the troll mask and chase you as you try to cross the bridge.

12. Free play! Use the remainder of the time as free play, allowing the children to explore storybook land as they choose.

Final Thoughts

Setting up a pretend storybook land is a great way to use the imagination and foster the developmental skills children need to grow and learn about the world around them. While learning about classic stories, children will also:

1. Use their imaginations while playing with storybook props to create a storybook land experience.

2. Develop thinking skills as they use items such as popsicle sticks, boxes, and paper bags for storybook play.

3. Enhance language skills by listening to stories and by engaging in conversation about various stories.

4. Build social skills by learning to share and converse with other children during storybook play.

5. Exercise motor skills as they participate in interactive songs and physical play such as building houses and escaping the troll.

Let's Pretend: A Rainy Day

Overview

Rain, rain, don't go away. It's so much fun to splash and play! Rather than treating a rainy day as a day that must be spent indoors, show children the fun that it can bring. "Let's Pretend: A Rainy Day" offers ideas on how to set up an imaginary rainy day using books, songs, props, and rain-related activities.

Figure 45.1. A perfect puddle for splashing

Materials Needed

Props

Puddles: blue poster board
Cut puddle shapes out of the poster board and secure to the floor with strong tape (see Figure 45.1).
Clouds: white poster board, stuffing (cotton craft batting), fishing line
Cut cloud shapes out of the poster board and cover with the stuffing. Hang the clouds around the room with the fishing line.
Rainbow: poster board, markers
Color a rainbow on the poster board and cut out the shape. Tape it to a table that can be crawled under.
Raindrops: aluminum foil
Cut raindrop shapes out of the aluminum foil and tape throughout the room.
Miscellaneous: rain boots, raincoats, umbrellas, spray bottle, rainstorm sound effects CD

Books

Bridges, Margaret Park. *I Love the Rain*. San Francisco: Chronical Books, 2005.

Music

Allard, Peter T., and Ellen Allard. "Hello Everybody." *Sing It! Say It! Stamp It! Sway It! Volume 1* [CD]. Worcester, MA: 80-Z Music, 1999.
Kaye, Mary. "Rain." *Mouse Jamboree* [CD]. 2004.

A Rainy Day: A Step-by-Step Program Example

1. Opening song: "Hello Everybody."
2. Talk with the children about rain. Ask them questions such as:
   - What are the different sounds rain makes?
   - How does rain change the way things look? (distorted looking through a window, shiny, etc.)
   - What do you wear in the rain?
3. Read *I Love the Rain*.
4. Listen to "Rain" as you drop "raindrops" around the circle and use a spray mist (lightly).
5. Let's play in the rain! Play a rainy nature sounds CD. Grab your raincoat and boots and lead children to the obstacle course.
6. A rainy obstacle: Show the children how to jump from puddle to puddle, jump up and touch a hanging cloud, and crawl through the rainbow. Let each child have a turn.
7. Free play! Use the remainder of the time for free play, allowing the children to splash in the puddles and enjoy this rainy day as they choose.

Final Thoughts

Setting up a pretend rainy day is a great way to use the imagination and foster the developmental skills children need to grow and learn about the world around them. While learning about rain and ways to play in it, children will also:

1. Use their imaginations while playing with props such as puddles to create a rainy-day experience.
2. Develop thinking skills as they use items such as umbrellas and aluminum foil for other purposes.
3. Enhance language skills by listening to a story and music and by engaging in conversation about rain.
4. Build social skills by learning to share and converse with other children during rainy day play.
5. Exercise motor skills as they participate in interactive songs and physical play such as puddle jumping.

Let's Pretend:
A Mystery

Overview

Get a clue and solve a mystery or two. It's time to bring out the magnifying glasses and become detectives. "Let's Pretend: A Mystery" offers ideas on how to introduce children to detective work and mysteries using a story, music, props, and mystery-related activities.

Materials Needed

Figure 46.1. Looking for clues!

Props

Magnifying Glass: cardboard
  Cut the shape of a magnifying glass out of cardboard. Be sure to cut the center out of the piece in order to look through it (see Figure 46.1).
Mystery Feely Boxes: box with lid, various items (rice, feathers, grapes, etc.)
  Cut a hole in the box big enough to fit a hand through. Place various items in the box. If the items are wet, line the box with cellophane.
Mystery Sound Boxes: box with lid, various items (marbles, beans, rice, etc.)
  Place various items in the box. Secure the lid for shaking.
Shape Mystery: construction paper, folder
  Make footprint/shoeprint shapes out of blue, red, and green construction paper. Cut out two blue squares, two red circles and two green triangles. Place one of each footprint/shoeprint color and shape in a folder. Hide the other shapes in/under various items (picture, book, box) and make a trail with the footprints/shoeprints. The children will follow the blue footprints/shoeprints to find the blue square, the red footprint/shoe print to find the red circle and the green footprints/shoeprints to find the green triangle.
Puzzle Mystery: picture of a puppy, box of toys (including a Frisbee), table of various empty food containers (including an empty Milkbone box), brown poster board cut to look like a mud puddle, folder, list of clues (Frisbee picture, Milkbone/bone picture, small mud puddle shape from construction paper)
  Cut three pieces out of the puppy picture. Tape the first piece under a Frisbee in the box of toys. Place the second piece in the Milkbone box on the table with the other food items. Place the third piece under the mud puddle.
Miscellaneous: disguises (hats, wigs, noses, etc.)

Books

Kellogg, Steven. *The Missing Mitten Mystery*. New York: Dial Books for Young Readers, 2000.

Marzollo, Jean. *I Spy* books. Various publishers and years.

Music

Allard, Peter T., and Ellen Allard. "Hello Everybody." *Sing It! Say It! Stamp It! Sway It! Volume 1* [CD]. Worcester, MA: 80-Z Music, 1999.

Sharon, Lois & Bram. "Every Great Detective." *Silly & Sweet Songs: Favourites from Our Hit T.V. Series!* [CD]. Toronto: Skinnamarink Entertainment, 1999.

A Mystery: A Step-by-Step Program Example

1. Opening song: "Hello Everybody."
2. Talk with the children about mysteries/detectives. Ask them questions such as:
   - What is a detective? (person who solves mysteries)
   - How does a detective solve a mystery? (gathers clues)
3. Read *The Missing Mitten Mystery*. Discuss how the mitten was found.
4. Use the magnifying glasses and listen to "Every Great Detective."
5. Play "I Spy."
6. Okay, detectives, we have work to do. Pull out a folder with the shapes and footprints/shoeprints. Explain that they have to follow the blue footprints/shoeprints to find the blue square, the red footprints/shoeprints to find the red circle, and the green footprints/shoeprints to find the green triangle. Grab your magnifying glasses and go!
7. More detective work! Pull out the folder with the puppy picture and clues. Tell them that they have to use the clues to find the missing pieces. Begin with clue #1: This animal likes to play fetch. Find the toy box and look for something that can be used for fetching. Once they find the first piece, give them the second clue: This animal likes bones. Find the food table and look for bone treats. After they find the second piece, give them the final clue: This animal like to play and dig in the mud. Find the mud puddle. Yay! The mystery picture has been solved. It's a puppy!
8. Free play! Use the remainder of the time for free play, allowing the children to dress in disguises, explore the mystery boxes, look at *I Spy* books, and play detective as they wish.

Final Thoughts

Playing detectives and solving mysteries is a great way to use the imagination and foster the developmental skills children need to grow and learn about the world around them. While learning about mysteries and detectives, children will also:

1. Use their imaginations while playing with props such as mystery boxes and clues to create a detective experience.
2. Develop thinking skills as they use clues to solve mysteries.
3. Enhance language skills by listening to a story and music and by engaging in conversation about mysteries and detectives.
4. Build social skills by learning to share and converse with other children during detective play.
5. Exercise motor skills as they participate in interactive songs and physical play such as looking for clues.

Let's Pretend: Recycling Center

Overview

Reduce, reuse, recycle. It's never too early to teach children the importance of these "Three R's" of the environment. "Let's Pretend: Recycling Center" provides ideas on how to introduce children to ways to help the environment while promoting creativity using a story, rhyme, props, and recycling-related activities.

Materials Needed

Props

Recycling Bins: 3 boxes, picture of can, paper, and plastic
Use three different boxes for recycling bins. Tape a picture of can(s) to the box for recycling cans, a picture of paper to the box for recycling paper, and a picture of plastic to the box for recycling plastic (see Figure 47.1).
Compost Bin: box
Trash: clean recyclables and yard waste
Have several bags of clean plastic, cans, paper, and yard waste that can be sorted and placed in the appropriate recycling bins and compost.
Reuse Center: table, craft supplies, trash that can be used to make some-thing (milk jugs, cans, boxes, toilet

Figure 47.1. Let's recycle!

paper rolls, magazine pictures, empty food containers, buttons, etc), including reused props from previous chapters such as toilet paper roll binoculars, food container drum, toy cast, etc., to provide ideas

Books

Wallace, Nancy Elizabeth. *Recycle Every Day!* Tarrytown, NY: Marshall Cavendish, 2003.

Music

Allard, Peter T., and Ellen Allard. "Hello Everybody." *Sing It! Say It! Stamp It! Sway It! Volume 1* [CD]. Worcester, MA: 80-Z Music, 1999.

Other

"Three Recycling Bins" (*Tune*: "Three Blind Mice")

Three recycling bins
Three recycling bins
For paper, plastic, and tin
For paper, plastic, and tin.
We sort our trash
And put it in the right space.
It makes the world a better place.
Three recycling bins
Three recycling bins.

Recycling Center: A Step-by-Step Program Example

1. Opening song: "Hello Everybody."
2. Talk with the children about recycling. Ask them questions such as:
   - How do you recycle trash?
   - Why is it important to recycle?
3. Read *Recycle Every Day!*
4. Encourage the children to join you in singing "Three Recycling Bins" while demonstrating what to do.
5. Let's recycle! Show the children the recycling and compost bins. Explain how to use them. Be sure to point out the pictures. Let the children sort through the trash bags and place the items in the appropriate bins.
6. Let's reuse it! Show the children things that can be made out of what would typically be put in the garbage (toilet paper binoculars, food container drum, toy cast, etc.). Let them make things out of the trash provided.
7. Free play! Use the remainder of the time for free play, allowing the children to sort more garbage and create more reusable things.

Final Thoughts

Showing children how to recycle garbage and reuse it is a great way to use the imagination and foster the developmental skills children need to grow and learn about the world around them. While learning about recycling, children will also:

1. Use their imaginations to create reusable things out of garbage such as toilet paper binoculars.
2. Develop thinking skills as they learn to sort garbage into the appropriate bins and find new ways to reuse garbage.
3. Enhance language skills by listening to a story and music and by engaging in conversation about recycling.
4. Build social skills by learning to share and converse with other children during recycling center play.
5. Exercise motor skills as they participate in interactive songs and physical play such as sorting and creating things.

Let's Pretend: Who Am I?

Overview

Children love to role-play and play dress-up. It's not only fun, it's good for their imaginations. "Let's Pretend: Who Am I?" offers ideas on how to use books, action rhymes, music, and props to encourage a variety of imaginative role-play.

Materials Needed

Props

Fairy Wings: cardboard, elastic, decorations
  Cut the wings out of cardboard. Attach elastic to each wing for straps. Decorate with paint, glitter, ribbons, etc.
Crowns: construction paper, glitter
  Cut a crown out of construction paper and decorate. Attach the two ends together.
Eye Patch: construction paper, elastic
  Cut a circle out of black construction paper and attach elastic (make it the correct size for a child's head).
Space Helmets: grocery bag, markers
  Turn the bag upside down and cut out a circle (about the size of a child's face) on the front. Decorate it with markers (see Figure 48.1).
Cape: pillowcase, yarn
  Attach a piece of yarn to each side of the pillowcase to wear as a cape.
Knight Costume: pillowcase, coat of arms picture
  Cut three holes in the pillowcase along the seam and sides for the head and arms. Cut rectangular shapes around the bottom. Glue a coat of arms picture to the front (see Figure 48.2).
Miscellaneous: animal masks, hats, old adult clothes, necklaces

Other

  Set up mirrors if possible. Add large appliance boxes, sheets, and other toys for play props, or use props made from previous programs.

Figure 48.1. We're astronauts!

Figure 48.2. I'm a knight!

Books

Brown, Lisa. *How to Be*. New York: HarperCollins Publishers, 2006.
Marzollo, Jean. *Pretend You're a Cat*. New York: Dial Books for Young Readers, 1990.

Music

Allard, Peter T., and Ellen Allard. "Hello Everybody." *Sing It! Say It! Stamp It! Sway It! Volume 1* [CD]. Worcester, MA: 80-Z Music, 1999.
Parachute Express. "World of Make-Believe." *Feel the Music* [CD]. Glendale, CA: Trio Lane Records, 1998.
Sharon, Lois & Bram. "Dressing Up." *Silly & Sweet Songs: Favourites from Our Hit T.V. Series!* [CD]. Toronto: Skinnamarink Entertainment, 1999.

Other

"I'm a Little Tea Pot"

"I'm a Little Popcorn Kernel"
I'm a little popcorn kernel, (*Sit on floor with arms around your knees in a ball.*)
Shaking to and fro, (*Rock back and forth.*)
When I get hot enough (*Uncurl slowly.*)
Pop! I go!

Who Am I? A Step-by-Step Program Example

1. Opening song: "Hello Everybody."
2. Talk with the children about pretending and dressing up. Ask them questions such as:
   - What do you like to pretend to be?
   - What is fun about dressing up?
3. Read *How to Be*.
4. Let the children join you in becoming a teapot and reciting "I'm a Little Teapot."
5. Let the children join you in becoming popcorn and reciting "I'm a Little Popcorn Kernel."
6. Read *Pretend You're a Cat*.
7. Listen/act out "World of Make-Believe."
8. Who do you want to be? Let the children choose a dress-up item.
9. It's the "Who Am I? Parade." Play "Dressing Up" and let the children parade around in their dress-up articles.
10. Free play! Use the remainder of the time for free play, allowing the children to play with the dress-up items and other props as they choose.

Final Thoughts

Role-playing and playing dress-up is a great way to use the imagination and foster the developmental skills children need to grow and learn about the world around them. While learning about how to take on a different role, children will also:

1. Use their imaginations to use props to become a desired persona.
2. Develop thinking skills as they consider the traits of different roles.

3. Enhance language skills by listening to stories and music and by engaging in conversation during role-play.
4. Build social skills by learning to share and converse with other children during role-play.
5. Exercise motor skills as they participate in interactive songs and physical play such as parading in costumes.

Let's Pretend: Where Am I?

Overview

Children love to pretend to be in different places. It doesn't take much effort to let their imaginations soar into a camping trip, bus ride, castle, or tea party. "Let's Pretend: Where Am I?" offers ideas on how to use books, action rhymes, music, and props to encourage a variety of imaginative play that will carry them to another place.

Figure 49.1. Let's go on a train ride!

Figure 49.2. Let's go on a bus ride!

Materials Needed

Props

Tent: blankets/sheets and chairs
Drape blankets and sheets over chairs to make a tent.

Train: 3 or more boxes (2 big enough for a child to sit in), rope, cardboard tube, white tissue paper, paper plates
Use a small box for the front of the train. Place the cardboard tube on top of it to make the "smokestack" and stuff the tissue paper inside the tube for "smoke." Use rope to connect the other boxes. Cut holes in the boxes for windows and doors. If you want the train to be able to "move," cut the bottom out of the boxes so that the children can walk around to make the train "run" (like a Flintstone car). Paint paper plates black and glue them to the boxes to make "wheels." Paint the train as you wish (see Figure 49.1).

City Bus: large box, paper plates
Use a large box to make a bus. Cut out windows and a door. Paint paper plates black and glue them to the bus for wheels. Paint the bus as you wish. If you want your bus to be mobile, cut the bottom out so that the children can walk around the room with it as they "drive" (see Figure 49.2).

Igloo: egg cartons or milk jugs
Glue egg cartons together and paint white (if needed) or glue milk jugs together in a circular or square shape, layered to desired height.

Boat: box (large enough for several children to fit in), 2 large pieces of cardboard, paint

Use the two large pieces of cardboard to make the bow of the boat by attaching them together (hot glue works well) and then attaching them to one end of the box. Paint the box as you wish and then paint "water" along the bottom of the box (see Figure 49.3).

Castle: box(es), rope

Cut rectangular crenellations along the top of the box(es). Cut out a drawbridge door on one side, leaving it attached to the box. Add a rope to each side of the door and adjoining wall. Cut window(s) on the other sides of the box(es). If you are attaching several boxes together to make a larger castle, cut out the interior walls of all three boxes, leaving enough cardboard to attach the boxes with brads (see Figure 49.4).

Airplane: large rectangular box, cardboard

Place the box lengthwise. Use the cardboard to make wings and attach to each side of the box. Cut holes or paint black circles on the sides for windows, and create an entrance (see Figure 49.5).

Tea Party Set: tea set, table and chairs (see Figure 29.1, p. 77)

Fishing Pond: blue poster board or butcher paper, construction paper, magnets, dowels, string, paper clips

Cut a large piece of poster board or butcher paper to look like the shape of a pond. Cut the paper into fish shapes. Glue a magnet on the back of each fish.

Figure 49.3. Let's go on a boat ride!

Figure 49.4. Let's visit a castle!

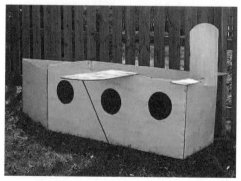

Figure 49.5. Let's go on a plane ride!

Place them in the "pond" (see Figure 1.2, p. 1). Tie a string around the end of the dowel. Tie a paperclip to the end of the string.

Books

Goennel, Heidi. *I Pretend*. New York: Tambourine Books, 1995.
Thomson, Sarah L. *Imagine a Day*. New York: Atheneum Books for Young Readers, 2005.

Music

Allard, Peter T., and Ellen Allard. "Hello Everybody." *Sing It! Say It! Stamp It! Sway It! Volume 1* [CD]. Worcester, MA: 80-Z Music, 1999.

Other

"Climbing Up the Apple Tree"

Climbing up the apple tree, (*Climb in place.*)
Swinging on a limb! (*Raise arms above head; sway left and right.*)
If I hear a robin, I may... (*Cup hand near ear.*)
Sing along with him! (*Sing "tra la la."*)
And Robin, if you fly away, (*Put hands over eyes.*)
Here's what I think I'll do. (*Point up with index finger.*)
I'll wish a pair of sparrow wings (*Gently flap arms at side and move around.*)
And fly away with you!

Let's Pretend: Where Am I? A Step-by-Step Program Example

1. Opening song: "Hello Everybody."
2. Talk with the children about pretending to be in other places. Ask them questions such as:
   - Where do you like to pretend to be or go?
   - What is fun about pretending to be in or go to another place?
3. Read *Imagine a Day*.
4. Encourage the children to join you in the action rhyme "Climbing Up the Apple Tree."
5. Read *I Pretend*.
6. Where do you want to go? Introduce the children to the location props (tent, igloo, castle, tea party, fishing pond).
7. How do you want to get there? Introduce the children to the transportation props and talk about where they could take them.
8. Free play! Use the remainder of the time for free play, allowing the children to travel by various means and to various places as they desire.

Final Thoughts

Pretending to be in different places and traveling by different means is a great way to use the imagination and foster the developmental skills children need to grow and learn about the world around them. While pretending to go different places, children will also:

1. Use their imaginations while playing with props such as pretend castles and trains.
2. Develop thinking skills as they consider the different places they want to go and different ways to travel and by using items such as boxes and sheets for other purposes.
3. Enhance language skills by listening to stories and music and by engaging in conversation during pretend play.
4. Build social skills by learning to share and converse with other children during pretend play.
5. Exercise motor skills as they participate in interactive songs/rhymes and physical play such as traveling to pretend places.

Let's Pretend: A World of Pure Imagination

Overview

Albert Einstein once said that "imagination is more important than knowledge." It's the beginning of how we come to know things. "Let's Pretend: A World of Pure Imagination" offers ideas on how to use books, rhymes, music, and props to encourage a variety of open-ended imaginative play.

Materials Needed

Props

Boxes: large appliance box and a variety of smaller-sized boxes (see Figure 50.1)
Linens: bedsheet, blankets, pillowcases (see Figure 50.2)
Cardboard Tubes: from paper towel and toilet paper rolls
Paper Plates
Tables and Chairs
Paper Bags
Empty Food Containers
Pie Pans
Egg Cartons
Dowels
Dress-up Clothes: hats, scarves, gloves, jewelry, masks, etc.
Ribbons
Streamers

Figure 50.1. Let's pretend—in a box!

Figure 50.2. Let's pretend—under a sheet!

Books

Portis, Antoinette. *Not a Box*. New York: HarperCollins Publishers, 2006.
Thomson, Sarah L. *Imagine a Place*. New York: Antheneum Books for Young Readers, 2008.

Music

Allard, Peter T., and Ellen Allard. "Hello Everybody." *Sing It! Say It! Stamp It! Sway It! Volume 1* [CD]. Worcester, MA: 80-Z Music, 1999.

Maroon 5. "Pure Imagination." *Mary Had a Little Amp* [CD]. New York: BMG Music Entertainment, 2004.

Other

"Guess Who?"

Growl, growl	No, pigs don't roar!
Thud, thud (*Slap floor.*)	Can a cow be wiggling my latch?
Roar, roar	No, cows don't scratch.
Who's that knocking at the door?	Roar, roar
Pound, pound (*Hit floor.*)	Scratch, scratch
Stamp, stamp	Growl, growl
Scratch, scratch (*Scratch floor.*)	It's not an owl (*"Hoot, hoot."*)
Who's that wiggling the latch?	I know who it can be
Can a pig be at my door? (*"Oink."*)	A friendly lion visiting me!

Pure Imagination: A Step-by-Step Program Example

1. Opening song: "Hello Everybody."
2. Talk with the children about pretending. Ask them questions such as:
   - How do you pretend?
   - What are some things you can pretend to be?
   - Where are some places you can pretend to go?
3. Read *Imagine a Place*.
4. Let's pretend a wild animal is visiting us. Recite "Guess Who?"
5. Read *Not a Box*.
6. Give the children ribbons and streamers to dance with as you play "Pure Imagination."
7. Free play! Use the remainder of the time for free play, allowing the children to use the hodgepodge of props to explore various ways to pretend.

Final Thoughts

Offering a hodgepodge of props/items is a great way to encourage children to use their imaginations and foster the developmental skills children need to grow and learn about the world around them. While pretending to go different places, children will also:

1. Use their imaginations while playing with a variety of props/items such as boxes and sheets.
2. Develop thinking skills as they consider the different places they want to go and different things they want to be and by using items such as boxes and sheets for other purposes.
3. Enhance language skills by listening to stories and music and by engaging in conversation during pretend play.
4. Build social skills by learning to share and converse with other children during pretend play.
5. Exercise motor skills as they participate in interactive songs/rhymes and physical play.

Index

Page numbers in bold indicate illustrations.

About the Author

Rebecca C. Bane is a former staff member of the Youth Services Department at the Greenville County Library System in Greenville, SC, where she started the dramatic play literacy program "Let's Pretend," and is also a former employee of the Horry County Library System in Myrtle Beach, SC. She attended Coastal Carolina University in Myrtle Beach, SC, and Nene University in Northampton, England, where she studied English Literature and Global Studies, focusing on the Humanities. Because of her love and fascination with language and literacy, she has worked with adults and children on literacy development at the library and while serving as an adult education instructor on the Horry County Literacy Council.

Bane has always been a creative thinker, engaging in imaginative play with her imaginary friend, Sandra, at a very young age. As she began working with youth after college, she was put back in touch with her inner child and became devoted to the connection between literacy and the imagination. She has published an article, "Let's Pretend: Exploring the Value of Dramatic Play at the Library," in *Children and Libraries*. These days, she finds herself devoted to fostering the development of her own children but stays connected with the library and education system, working part-time as a substitute for the Greenville County (SC) Library System and serving as a Library Liaison for South Carolina Connections Academy, with a little photography on the side.